It isn't magic, it isn't all creativity and inspiration. It's work.

-- Laurie Pawlik-Kienlen, theadventurouswriter.com

to the
Boating Magazines
(and other niche mags)

Michael Robertson

Force Four | Publications

Selling Your Writing to the Boating Magazines (and other niche mags)

Force Four Publications
411 Walnut St. #8630
Green Cove Springs, FL 32043
www.forcefourpubs.com

PUBLISHER'S CATALOGING-IN-PUBLICATION DATA

NAMES: Robertson, Michael (1968-), author.
Title: Selling your writing to the boating magazines (and other niche mags). / Michael Robertson.
DESCRIPTION: First trade paperback original edition. | Green Cove Springs [Florida] : Force Four Publications, 2016. | Includes index.
IDENTIFIERS: ISBN 978-0-9971358-0-0 (pbk) | ISBN 978-0-9971358-1-7 (eBook)
SUBJECTS: LCSH: Freelance journalism. | Feature writing. | Feature writing---Vocational guidance. | Journalism---Authorship. | BISAC: LANGUAGE ARTS & DISCIPLINES / Journalism.
CLASSIFICATION: LCC 2015921023 | DDC 808.02–dc23

FONTS USED IN THIS BOOK:

Angelina (courtesy of Angie Durbin)
Aparajita (developed by Modular Infotech)
Bohemian Typewriter (courtesy of Lukas Krakora at Dafont.com)
Calibri (designed by Lucas de Groot)
Garamond (named for Claude Garamont)
Type Keys Filled (courtesy of Ronna at Typadelic Fonts)

QUOTES USED BY PERMISSION:

Paula Biles of Seaworthy Goods, 53-54
Gary "Cap'n Fatty" Goodlander, 77
Karen Larson of Good Old Boat magazine, 33, 53-54
Tanya Loranca, 60
Laurie Pawlik-Kienlen, i, 3
Pat Schulte, 56-57
Diane Selkirk, 40

The author assumes all responsibility for errors or omissions.

Printed in the United States of America

To Windy, Eleanor, and Frances

Acknowledgments

The solitary act of writing is just a part of the effort required to produce a finished book. My thanks and appreciation go to the following individuals who supported my efforts to produce and launch this one: Paula Biles, Jen Brett, Behan Gifford, Gary "Cap'n Fatty" Goodlander, Sara Dawn Johnson, Karen Larson, Beth Leonard, Tanya Loranca, Eleanor Merrill, Lin Pardey, Laurie Pawlik-Kienlen, Tim Queeney, Windy Robertson, Pat Schulte, and Diane Selkirk.

Contents

Introduction 1

The Lingo 4

The Idea 10

The Magazine 31

The Writing.. 39

The Photos.. 47

The Query & Pitch.. 62

The Submission 78

The Money.. 85

Appendix: Boating Mag Market 89

Index.. 96

About The Author 100

Introduction

So you want to sell your writing to the boating magazines? Or perhaps to the camping, climbing, or cat-lover magazines? Maybe the knitting, kiting, or kayaking magazines? Or the gambling, golfing, or gardening magazines? The parenting, papyrus-making, or parachuting magazines? The flying, hot-rodding, R/C modeling, surfing, skiing, or photography magazines? You can sell your writing to any of these niche-market magazines, as long as…

- You are an enthusiast and can identify a magazine that caters to your special interest.

- You like to write and you are willing to take seriously the craft of writing and the business of selling writing.

That is it. You can do it. I am convinced everyone has a publishable story to write. There is work and dedication involved, but the path to publication is straightforward. Your success will not hinge on how many editors are your Facebook friends, or even how talented a writer you are. Your success will depend only on how much you want it.

In the chapters that follow I include all the information a writing-loving enthusiast needs to become a published writer. This is information I have gained—and lessons I have learned—over the past several years that I have spent writing and selling my stories to magazines.

Because I am a boater, my experiences are based on selling my writing to the boating magazines. In this book, through example and anecdote, I focus on that market. However, all the lessons I share here apply to selling words and pictures to any niche-market magazine.

Why niche-market magazines?

As a writer, all you have to sell are ordinary words that are free of charge and available to anyone. Of course, what matters are the words you choose and the order you choose to put them in. Moreover, there are many people like you, playing with ordinary words, trying to put them into an order that tells a story others want to read, and then selling them. Fortunately, you are entering a market that favors the freelance writer. That you are a freelance writer getting started means you are a freelance writer with a fresh voice.

Freelance writers produce a high percentage of the content in niche-market magazines. This is because these magazines' budgets and staffs are smaller than those of mainstream magazines. It is more cost-efficient to buy stories from freelance writers than to hire staff writers.

Writing repeatedly for magazines within a single niche-market means you gain name recognition quickly within your niche.

Additionally, the nature of many niche-market magazines is that they cover interests that are common to a small percentage of the population and it is a population that is interested in learning about other members and how they are exploring the same interest. In other words, readers of *People* magazine are not interested in other readers of *People* magazine and do not want to read articles written by other readers of *People* magazine. However, readers of *Model Railroader* are keen to read the words of a fellow model train enthusiast, just as a reader of *Yachting Monthly* will give great attention to a sailing yarn spun by a fellow sailor. *The New Yorker, The Atlantic, People,* and *Popular Science* might not need you, but the niche-market magazines do need you. You, aspiring niche-market magazine writer, have it good. You have a market, an avenue to selling your writing.

But as they say, "Wait! There's more."

Writing for magazines within a single niche means you gain name recognition quickly within your market. It means your story ideas are likely to feed off and build on one another. It means your knowledge of the subject matter builds on itself.

Writer Laurie Pawlik-Kienlen (theadventurouswriter.com) has sold stories to both mass-market and niche-market magazines. She focuses on the health sector and makes a good case for the focused approach. "The more you write about one particular niche or beat, the easier it is to research and write the article. For instance, I write health articles for *women's* magazine (published by the BC Women's Hospital). Every article I write teaches me more about medicine, medical terms, and health news, which makes me a better health writer. It's an upward spiral!"

Finally, niche-market magazines in general comprise a stable, healthy market to which to sell your writing. Because niche-market magazine content is focused, the audience is narrow—in some cases very narrow—and passionate. This is a readership that advertisers love and are willing to pay a premium to reach. Contrast this market to that of the mass-market, general-interest pubs available at super-market checkouts. The broad-appeal magazines enjoy much larger circulations, but those circulations are generally in decline. They are increasingly under threat from other media sources that feature the same broad-appeal content. What's a magazine going to tell you about the East Coast train derailment or the celebrity break-up that you haven't already seen reported online—and that you've read for free? The mass-market magazines do not have advertisers who will stick with them through thick and thin; Ford and Folgers can advertise anywhere. However, the company that manufactures the tiny trees and lampposts that model railroaders love, they are loyal to *Model Railroader* magazine.

The Lingo

K now the lingo. In the magazine writing business—as in just about any business—knowledge of the associated vocabulary is important. While a glossary is usually stuck in the back pages, apart from the content, in this book I have put it right here at the start. Following are definitions of the few terms you should know before you dive into this book, and certainly before you try to sell your words. At the very least skim through the alphabetized list and make sure everything is familiar.

Article: This is the name of the finished product, your story published and in print. It is the sum of your words, your pictures, the editor's edits, and the art director's formatting. Try not to refer to your **story** or **piece** as an **article** until it is indeed an **article**.

Artwork: Any part of a magazine that is not text.

Back of book: Most publishers structure their magazine in a similar manner. There is **front of book** content, **well** content, and **back of book** content. **Back of book** content is often comprised of advertising (both display and classified), shorter stories, and single-page columns.

Book: This is how some magazine editors refer to the product they assemble each month. Each issue of their magazine is a **book**.

Byline: This is your name, as it appears in print at the beginning or end of your **article**. If an editor or anyone else ever asks whether you have bylines, they are simply asking whether you have been published.

Circulation: The number of copies of each issue of a magazine that are distributed (either in print or digital form). I present **circulations** of various boating titles later in this book.

Clean copy: Story text (copy) that is edited, proofread, and ready to be typeset.

Column: A part of a magazine that is located in the same place every month and that uses the same heading. In each issue, the **column story** is usually (but not always) written by the same writer. This writer may be a staff writer or a freelancer.

Copyright: As soon as you write something you automatically, by law, own the **copyright** to that work. As the **copyright** holder, you alone decide what happens to it. You can set your work on fire or you can sell a publisher rights to produce and distribute your work. You can limit a publisher's rights to a geographic area or to a period of time. You can allow a publisher may use your work only online or only in print, or both. So long as you retain **copyright**, you retain the right to lay claim to being the creator of the work, regardless of what usage rights you sell.

Editor: These magazine employees are the gatekeepers who decide what content comprises each issue. The very smallest magazines (in terms of **circulation**) may list only one **editor** on the **masthead**. Most, even those with relatively modest **circulations**, employ multiple **editors**, each responsible for different content. It is the magazine **editor** with whom you will work—to whom you will try to sell your **story** ideas.

Feature: The longest **stories** in any magazine, the ones often called out on the cover, are the **feature** stories. **Feature stories** usually run between 1,500 and 3,000 words and the writers who produce them earn the highest fees.

First North American rights: These are the rights that most North American magazine editors want to buy from you. Purchasing these rights gives them the right to be the first publication to print your story among North American publications. Some contracts may specify a period (usually six months to a year) during which you may not offer your story to another publication. After any specified period, you are free to sell to anyone else the right to publish your story. However, note that you can sell *first North American* **rights** only one time. Publishers refer to any subsequent rights as reprint rights and they are, of course, less desirable. Also, note that you are never selling or relinquishing your **copyright**, unless you do so explicitly.

Front of book: Most publishers structure their magazines in a similar manner. There is **front of book** content, **well** content, and **back of book** content. **Front of book** is where you will find the **front matter** and sections of very short pieces. These pieces can include book or product reviews, news items, a featured photograph, and other tidbits. This is an excellent place for freelance writers to get started selling their writing.

Front matter: The pages of a magazine before the month's article content begins, in which full-page display ads, the table of contents, **masthead**, reader letters, a cover photo credit, and the editor's letter to readers are contained. All the **front matter** elements are contained within the part of a magazine called **front of book**.

Kill fee: When an editor rejects a story they contracted you to write, the editor will likely pay you a **kill fee**. This is the editor's way out of the agreement you had. This is payment for your trouble and frees you up to sell the story elsewhere. You may go your entire writing career and never come across a scenario requiring a **kill fee**.

Manuscript: This is your story in document form, as submitted.

Masthead: Publishers list magazine staff by name and title in a narrow column in the **front matter** of a magazine.

Media kit: Often available online, a magazine's **media kit** is a digest of information important to potential advertisers. This may include the magazine's reader demographic, distribution information, and editorial focus (sometimes with a high-level editorial calendar for the year). In this latter content, the freelance writer may find value.

On spec: If an **editor** tells you they would like you to submit a **story on spec**, it means they are interested in the idea you proposed, but they aren't willing to commit. In other words, "Feel free to write and send your **story**, your idea sounds good, but I'm not guaranteeing you I'll buy it." An **editor** may do this because either 1) they can imagine a great **story** coming from your idea, but they don't know whether you have the chops to write it, or 2) they have faith in your writing ability, but aren't certain your idea can be turned into a **story** they want to buy. In either case, you are risking only your time. Moreover, if an **editor** rejects a **story** they invited you to submit **on spec**, they should take the time to explain to you why. Having written **on spec**, you deserve this much.

Over the transom: This means unsolicited. I imagine an **editor** shouting over a cubicle to a colleague: "Hey Beth, I just got this great story **over the transom**." It is worth noting that this term is not boating magazine-specific.

Piece: This term is synonymous with **story**; **editors** use both to refer to your submitted manuscript. In my experience, **editors** favor **piece** when referring to very short submissions, such as a 175-word news item.

Pitch: I think of **pitch** as the act of trying to sell your idea for a **story** to an **editor**. Therefore, I tend to use **pitch** as a verb. "Hi Jen, I've been really busy these past few months getting ready for our Pacific crossing, but I have some great ideas to **pitch** once things settle down." I often hear it used as a noun too.

Pull quote: Ever read a magazine **article** and see a sentence repeated in a block in the middle of the **article** text in a font that is 3 to 4 times the size of the body text? The term for this block of called-out text is **pull quote**. I include **pull quotes** throughout this book.

Query: This is the actual text you send to an **editor** to sell your idea for a **story**. I tend to use **query** as a noun. "Hi Tim, I'm writing to ask whether you've had a chance to review the 'Readying your Boat to Cross the Pacific' **query** I sent last month." I often hear it used as a verb too.

Royalties: Do not ever use this word with regard to selling your **story** to a magazine. This is a book publishing word. Magazines will pay you a fee for your work they buy, never **royalties**.

Section: Magazines are highly structured, their contents organized into **sections**, one or more pages of contiguous content that is the responsibility of a single editor and that appears in the same part of the magazine each month (such as in the **front of book**, **well**, or **back of book**). Magazine **sections** change infrequently. **Editors** see each future issue as a template they have to fill. They are on the hunt for compelling content to fill each **section**. Your job as a writer is to view magazines the same way. What reader-pleasing content can you produce that will fit in what **section**?

Sidebar: A brief distillation of information relevant to your main **story**. In magazines, **sidebars** are text complimentary to the **article** and set off from the body of the **article** with a box or color or different font. Sometimes an **editor** will ask you to include with your manuscript a **sidebar** of specific information relevant to your **story**. For example, imagine you **pitched** an idea for a **story** about introducing non-sailing friends and family to the joy of sailing. The **editor** may respond, "I love your idea and can't wait to see your **story**, but please include a brief **sidebar** on the three most effective means of preventing sea sickness."

Story: This is the term most **editors** will use to refer to the text you propose to deliver or have delivered. You should use it too. It is nearly synonymous with **piece**. If the term sounds misleading because you think a **story** is something that starts, "It was a dark and stormy night..." or "Once upon a time..."—let it go. That 700-word, step-by-step instructional **article** you saw in *SAIL* magazine about adjusting a Monitor wind vane? It was a **story** first.

Upon acceptance: This term is related to payments and synonymous with **upon submission**. An **editor** who offers you, "$500 for your story, **upon acceptance**," is telling you to expect a check right around the time the **editor** accepts your submission. Obviously, this is the best-case scenario.

Upon publication: This term relates to payments. An **editor** who offers you, "$500 for your story, **upon publication**," is telling you to expect a check right around the time the issue that features your **story** hits the street. Do not be surprised if this is six months to a year (or more!) after the **editor** accepts your submission.

Upon submission: This term is related to payments and synonymous with **upon acceptance**. An **editor** who offers you, "$500 for your story, **upon submission**," is telling you to expect a check right around the time the **editor** accepts your submission.

Well: Most publishers structure their magazine in a similar manner. There is **front of book** content, **well** content, and **back of book** content. The **well** is the heart of a magazine, usually in the center of the **book**, and comprised of **feature**-length content (the major **articles** editors usually highlight on the cover) and few advertisements.

Word count: This is the number of words in your story. Microsoft Word (for example) makes it easy to determine **word count** (check out your document properties if you don't see a **word count** on screen—note that you can also view the **word count** of a highlighted portion of a Word document). Learn how to determine the **word count** in the word processing application you use. If an **editor** gives you a **word count** not to exceed, do not exceed it.

The Idea

No matter how many stories I've sold to magazines, no matter how much I improve as a writer, no matter how hard I work, no matter the strength of the working relationships I develop with editors, every story I sell is like starting over. Because every story must still begin with a new idea that has to come from me. No idea, no story.

Some writers always seem to have a dozen stories they are chomping at the bit to write and sell. Others not so much. For me, coming up with a saleable story idea is the biggest roadblock I will face on the path to finally picking up that magazine issue with my name and words inside. What in the world should I write about? That question always looms large. However, this idea hurdle gets easier to clear with time. It is a matter of developing a mindset whereby you consider all facets of your life and thoughts and experiences as potential story fodder. Successful writers have learned to recognize the good story ideas.

Successful writers have learned to recognize the good story ideas.

I will give you an example.

Years ago, around the time I was starting to consistently sell my writing to the boating magazines, I was having dinner with new friends. Sitting around their fireplace afterward, they told a story of how their 40-foot sloop had gone ashore during a strong Pacific Northwest storm. They were aboard at the time, along with their young daughter and the family dog. Everyone survived unscathed and their insurance company recovered and repaired their boat in the months that followed. Our friends pulled out a photo album dedicated to the episode and the pictures were as dramatic as their story.

A few months after our dinner, they wrote about the event on their family blog. Six months after that, their story was published in a national sailing magazine—written by a savvier, more prolific writing friend of mine who'd seen the blog post and contacted the family for an interview.

How had I completely missed the boat? That story was mine for the writing.

The answer is that I was not in the writer's mindset. I was not yet thinking about the things I was hearing and experiencing in the context of a story I could potentially write and sell. That's key. Pick up a magazine in your niche and look at all of the stories inside. How many of them are already familiar to you? How many of those stories are you as qualified to have written as the writer whose name is there on the page in black and white?

Stop missing those opportunities. I cannot get into your head and help you find story ideas, but I can help with the following tips, each inspired by my own experiences.

✎ **Read the magazines in which you hope to be published.** You really have to do this. As in any business, you need to know the market to which you are selling. Reading, even studying, the magazines to which you hope to sell is how you get to know the market. And knowing the market will serve to inspire story ideas. If knitting is your beat, subscribe to all the knitting magazines out there (or get your hands on some back issues). Read them with a critical eye. Notice the names of the freelance writers whose work appears regularly. What are they doing right? Can you do the same? Could their story idea have been yours?

I once read a short article in *Cruising World* magazine about one sailor's experience feeding the stingrays in French Polynesia. "Where the Rays Roam" was about 300 words long, featured a single photo, and appeared in the Underway section of the magazine. While I read, I saw parallels to a recent experience I'd had: seeing and touching gray whales and their calves from a *panga* in the birthing lagoon of Mexico's Bahia Magdalena. I fired off a query to the editor of the Underway section. I wrote that I had read "Where the Rays Roam" and that I had a similar, compelling story to offer. I called my story, "Where the Grays Go." She loved the idea and when I submitted my story a week later, she bought it.

🖋 **Stay in the magazine-story-idea mindset and keep your eyes open.** A friend of mine was in a Toys-Я-Us store and spotted a PLAYMOBIL playset featuring a PLAYMOBIL family in a lifeboat, part of a series of real-life adventure toys for kids. She thought it was absurd and hilarious, snapped a photo of the box with her smartphone, and emailed it to me for laughs. I too thought it was absurd and hilarious and then I realized that boating magazine readers would feel the same way. I forwarded the photo to a magazine editor with a note telling her how I felt about the photo and offering to write a short humorous piece. She told me to go ahead.

🖋 **What is unique about your circumstances?** The first story I ever sold was to *SAIL* magazine. It was a feature-length story about cruising on a shoestring budget in my twenties, falling in love with my crew, and later marrying her. It was an obvious life experience to write about. What about you? Are you a traveling retired teacher, sending dispatches back to kids in classrooms? Are you dropping in at the same anchorages that Graham, Aebi, Moitessier, and Roth stopped at, contrasting the voyage you are on with the voyages that inspired you? Are you a veterinarian/ophthalmologist/dentist lending your expertise to small communities along your path? Many sailors have fascinated me with their unique stories (I have even written and sold a few of these stories). Identify the thing that makes your journey (or someone else's journey) unique and then consider writing about it. If you

> *Identify the thing that makes your journey (or someone else's journey) unique and then consider writing about it.*

are boating in a remote location, you are the closest thing to an expert on boating in that time and place, period. If you are sailing with babies aboard, you are a member of an interesting minority. If you are out on the water and immersed in the boating world, chances are you are having unique experiences (or have a unique take on common experiences) that are fodder for saleable story ideas. You simply have to identify them. If you are inclined to write from these unique perspectives, you have a good shot at selling your work.

✎ **What are you learning or what do you want to know?** With a long motoring trip planned in our sailboat (up the Inside Passage from British Columbia to Alaska), I needed to learn to calculate the exact fuel consumption rate for our old Yanmar auxiliary. I turned to the Yanmar manual. Inside I found a few charts and a power curve graph. I realized all the data was there, but it was not presented in an accessible way. I wrote some equations, got out the calculator, crunched some numbers, put in some variables, and came up with the information I wanted: the amount of fuel burned per hour at a given RPM. With this info, I made a laminated chart for my nav station that lists, for specific RPM, the horsepower generated, the fuel burn rate, and the boat's speed in flat, still water. Figuring *Ocean Navigator* readers might be interested in learning the same about their motors, I sent my query and sold the story.

Another time, surfing the web, I stumbled on an article written by Peter Smith, the inventor of the Rocna anchor. In his article, Peter explained his controversial idea that, except in very deep water, the catenary provided by heavy, all-chain rode does not provide a benefit that warrants carrying that weight. He wrote that in very high winds, when holding is paramount, the rode will be drawn tight regardless of composition and therefore, scope is all that matters. This was a new and interesting idea to me, and I thought it might be as unfamiliar and interesting to *Pacific Yachting* readers. I pitched and sold a story in which I shared what I learned from reading Peter Smith's ideas.

What questions are people asking you? There may be no greater indicator of the knowledge and perspectives you possess—and that others seek—than the questions people ask you. Several sailors have asked me how they should go about selling their stories to the sailing magazines. Their questions are what sparked the idea for this book. If you have a blog, what are readers asking? When my wife and I began cruising again in our forties, with our two young daughters, the question friends and strangers most often asked was: "How did you do it? How were you able to afford to jump out of the rat race at that time in your life when you're supposed to be tending to your house, kids, and career?" I had been reading *Cruising World* and I knew they had not run an article that answered these questions, so I pitched one to an editor there. I wrote in my query that I would interview five cruising families, learn how they did it, and write a story based on those answers. I wrote that I would include a photo of each family I interviewed. The editor told me to go ahead. I interviewed five families, wrote my story, and submitted it.

What surprises are delighting you (or what are the go-to stories from your life you like to share)? Days before we dropped the hook off Mexico's remote and tiny Islas San Benitos in 2013, I began thinking of the time I was last there, almost twenty years before. About an hour before we dropped the hook, it occurred to me that I had digitized photos from that long-ago trip stored on a hard drive aboard, photos of people we met on that first trip. Wouldn't it be fun to…yes it would. I found the pictures on the hard drive and fired up our printer.

When we landed, I showed the printed pictures to the first people we met and we soon had a crowd gathered around us. Then, an elderly woman pulled me aside to tell me that one of the young boys in my pictures was her son. He was doing well, working in a fish camp on an island 80 miles away; she did not see him often. She asked if she could have the photo. I asked if I could take her picture holding the photo. Later, after looking at the picture I took of the woman and after sharing that story with several people, I realized what a great story it was and I pitched it and sold it.

✎ **What is happening in the world around you?** On three serendipitous occasions, I got a writing assignment: *Cruising World* asked me to review a cruising guide for an area I had just explored, *Good Old Boat* asked me to cover a yacht race happening where I happened to be, and then *Cruising World* asked for a report on a hurricane that struck an area I was near. This serendipity was only possible because I had already sold stories to those editors and formed relationships with them. I was in contact and they knew where I was at the time. However, note the last two examples. In those cases, I simply happened to be where something of interest to the magazines was occurring. I was fortunate to have the editor relationships I did, but if I had not, my location would have been a great segue to pitch the same stories. What is happening around you that might be of interest to the magazines? Niche-market magazines usually do not have the staff resources to send reporters to where the action is. If you are where the action is, do not delay! Start taking pictures, writing queries, and reaching out. Unleash your inner journalist!

I hope those thoughts and anecdotes help you to generate your own story ideas. However, do not chase just any idea that pops into your head. Remember that the best stories are going to be the ones you want to write, the ones you are motivated to write. Learn to recognize that feeling in yourself, the one that distinguishes an idea from a good idea that excites you. A saleable story idea in the hands of a writer not interested in that story probably will not end up being a well-written story. Know yourself. If you enjoy writing about the technical side of life, do not try to wax poetic about the sunsets that wowed you on a 4-day passage. Instead, give your idea a twist so that it becomes something you are eager to explore and share. Perhaps learn about the green flash, what it is and the atmospheric conditions necessary to see one. Then write a story that shares your technical knowledge and perspective in the context of your recent passage, and the green flash the crew waited hopefully to see each evening.

> *Know yourself. If you enjoy writing about the technical side of life, do not try to wax poetic about the sunsets that wowed you on a 4-day passage.*

In addition, an idea for a story does not necessarily have to be current to be relevant or saleable. I see articles all the time from cruising sailors describing adventures I know occurred years before. Of course, some ideas do not age well and will be stale no matter how you write them. However, if you have a good story from long ago, consider whether it still holds appeal.

Breaking and Entering

The question that unpublished writers who want to start selling their writing ask me most often is: *Where is the best place to break in?* I think the best place to break in is where demand for freelancer services is highest.

Many years ago, when she was the Managing Editor of *SAIL* magazine, Amy Ullrich told me that, "short pieces are especially prized." I had just sold her my first feature story and (eager to sound professional) I had asked about her, "editorial needs." I have since learned the value of her answer.

Most magazine editors are on a perpetual hunt for short and informative pieces they can use to fill their front-of-the-book sections. These stories serve to grab the short attention spans of newsstand browsers and they remind subscribers that the magazine is a fresh, timely source of information related to the particular niche. Study the front-of-the-book sections of your favorite magazines. Learn how the magazine organizes this content, who is producing this content (in-house editors or freelancers—or both), and what type of content they feature. You should get a good idea of what a magazine editor is looking for—and likely to buy—based on your study. What can you produce along the same lines? (I will note that with regard to payment, these shorter stories do not pay much, but can be especially lucrative on a fee-per-word basis.)

Selling these shorter stories is a good way of getting your foot in the proverbial door. Think of these 50- to 500-word articles as your opportunities. Event announcements, death notices, book reviews, product reviews, recipes, one-page destination pieces, and news items related to the boating world. It is a senior editor's burden to fill these front-of-the-book sections each month. You can help her.

The front of the book is the most common place for these pieces, but not every magazine is structured conventionally. For example, *Good Old Boat* does not have a front of the book section filled with short pieces. Rather, they spread short pieces throughout the book. *Good Old Boat* also features an extensive reader mail section called Mail Buoy that is unusual in that it includes not just the standard reader feedback, but also includes anecdotes, reflections, and tips that can include photos and run up to 300 words. Get to know the nuances of the magazines you aim to sell to. This knowledge will help you to write better-targeted pitches and maybe spark story ideas.

> *I think the best place to break in is where demand for freelancer services is highest.*

Several of the boating magazines I know feature a column specifically reserved for freelancer/reader stories—or at least a new writer each month. This is common among niche publications in particular because readers enjoy learning from fellow enthusiasts. These columns are good places to break in as the parameters of the content are defined and you can study past columns to get a feel for the writing they have published and compare it to your own work. *SAIL* runs an Experience column in which they publish readers' stories of mishap and lessons learned. *Good Old Boat* prints a similar column for reader stories called Learning Experience. In addition, both these magazines feature other columns written by freelancers: Cruising Memories and Reflections in *Good Old Boat* and Windshifts in *SAIL*.

One very specific avenue for writers looking for their first byline and the opportunity to develop a working relationship with an editor is a book review. Most niche magazines publish reviews of books written about the respective subject area. In many cases, a small number of freelance writers writes these reviews. Why not you? I write about writing book reviews under the next subheading, "What Kind of Story?"

Finally, consider breaking in at smaller magazines. Small waterfront newspapers, for example, may not pay much (sometimes nothing) and their editorial focus is usually narrow and local, but if you have a suitable story, these publications may be a good place to get a byline under your belt. Also, consider online-only boating magazines, such as:

Sail-World (worldwide, news oriented, online article submission form)

Sailing Anarchy (tell-it-like-it-is focused, online article submission form)

Scuttlebutt Sailing News (North America focused, news oriented, "If you have a story, a photo, an idea…contact us.")

SSCA Commodore's Bulletin and **Additional Publications** (membership organization, cruising sailor focused, member submissions only)

Small Boats Monthly ("Dedicated to owners and users of wooden boats that can be stored and maintained at an average-size home.")

Three Sheets Northwest (Pacific Northwest focused, "*Three Sheets Northwest* is always looking for good stories, whether they're ones we write ourselves or stories contributed by readers")

What Type of Story?

Which *types* of stories are you eager to write? Consider the following story types. They may help you generate new story ideas, or perhaps they may give a new spin to an idea you have not yet been able to see as a story.

🖉 **About a Person** This is one of my favorite types of stories to write. When I have come across (or reached out to) a boater who has inspired me or who fascinates me, I know I have a saleable story. People like reading about interesting people. Writing about them is fun because you can let your own enthusiasm bleed through your writing.

When I read that 70-year-old Jeanne Socrates was going to be in the same city I was going to be in, starting her third attempt at a solo circumnavigation, I sent her an email. I said I would like to interview her for a magazine story. She said yes. I spent 10 days working alongside her, helping her ready her boat for the trip, listening to her stories, and asking questions as they occurred to me.

It's best to know where you're going to try and sell your profile—or sell it before you start—because for this type of story, you're taking someone else's time and they're likely presuming your story will be published. I do not want to discourage you, but I do want to encourage you to try to find a home for your story before you get started. Failing this (or absent the time to do this), I would make sure your subject knows you're writing on spec, that you have a few publications in mind for the story, but no commitment yet from any of them.

Your perspective of a place should be unique and your writing should make the reader wish they were there (or glad they are not).

Another thing to be aware of is that some magazines have a rigid format for profile stories. If you write a great story, but then learn the magazine publishes profiles only in a Q&A format, you may be out of luck (for that publication).

Finally, this story type—among the easiest to sell—is unique among all of them because it usually requires an interview. I was very nervous the first time I formally interviewed someone for a story, a couple of French acrobats who performed aboard their boat. *Who died and made me a writer? They're gonna see right through me and know I'm not a real journalist. Are my questions lame or inappropriate? Oh no, they're talking so fast and am I taking too long to jot down their answers and are they getting impatient?* Despite my insecurities, this first experience turned out fine.

Your first experience will go well too. Start by imagining the story you intend to write—the one you would like to read—and determine the questions you need answered to write that story. Do your homework to learn about your subject before you meet. This will increase your comfort level going into the interview and allow you to come up with questions that are informed and interesting. Write your questions down beforehand.

Try to conduct the interview on your subject's turf (they may have a picture on their wall that sparks questions or a story, they may be moved to show you something interesting). Regardless of where you conduct your interview, begin noting details about the environment as soon as your arrive. You may be able to use those details to add color to your story. When you ask your questions, don't give so much attention to transcribing answers that you forget to really listen to those answers—or that you miss visual cues from the subject. Recording an interview is an effective way to eliminate the distraction that transcribing can introduce. But even if you record your interview (smartphones are great for this), take at least high-level notes that you can use to jog your memory in the event you have a technical problem.

Finally, when your interview is over, ask permission to follow-up later—you will likely need clarification on some things as you start to write. Do your best and have fun!

The parallel for magazines in other niches: These stories are about subjects readers are keen to know more about. This can be either a person already known to readers, or a person readers would want to know about.

About a Place Before writing about a place, be sure you can accompany your story with quality photos. Your perspective of a place should be unique and your writing should make the reader wish they were there (or glad they are not). Remember that while your trip to Catalina Island was thrilling, it is only 25 miles off the coast of Southern California and vis-

> *Remember that if you are interested enough in writing to pick up this book, you are a writer.*

ited by thousands and thousands of boaters each year. Consider how your story could be a unique take on this landmark. Ask yourself: Why should readers care?

There are challenges facing a writer writing about an oft-visited, well-known place, however, they are not insurmountable. Maybe think about re-categorizing your story, perhaps as a List type of story (see below): "Top 5 Attractions for Sailors on Catalina Island." Even if I had been there a dozen times, I would want to read that article. I will bet an editor would see it the same way. Destination stories are often features, but can also be very short. *Cruising World, Powerboat Cruising, Pacific Yachting,* and *Blue Water Sailing* are the boating magazines I know are most receptive to destination stories. Many other boating magazines, such as *SAIL, Boating,* and *BoatU.S.* feature narrower-scope stories in this vein, perhaps written with a twist so that it is not a story purely about the destination, but what you discovered there.

> *The parallel for magazines in other niches: So imagine you are a knitting writer wanting to write for* Creative Knitting *magazine. You are on a trip to Scotland or Ireland to celebrate your wedding anniversary. You stumble upon a loom museum or maybe the town where the sheep produce the finest wool in the world. If the museum or town interests you, it should interest your fellow enthusiasts. Get out your camera and start taking notes.*

✎ **Environmental Slant** Any short piece that relates your niche and the environment is especially saleable these days. *Cruising World* magazine features a 300-word section in the front of the book each month called Green Wakes that is reserved for just these stories. Editors of other magazines without a column are just as eager to include these types of stories. Keep your ears and eyes open.

✎ **Recipes and Food-Related** Not all boating magazines feature recipes or cover food, many of them do. Do you like to cook?

✎ **More Picture than Words** There are times when I've gotten lucky with my camera and wound up with a picture that is stunning—and I have no significant or saleable story to accompany it. Do not despair if this happens to you. The writer's guidelines of many magazines say explicitly that they are always interested in great photos alone.

If your great photo is attention grabbing, of portrait orientation, and features space in the right places (to allow for the title of the magazine and for text highlighting the contents), it may be a great cover photo.

Alternatively, a great landscape shot, perhaps with a short story reflecting on the circumstances of the photo or on the nature of life itself, might be appropriate for the front of the book of some magazines. *Cruising World*, *SAIL*, and *BoatU.S.* each feature such a photo every month. Even if a magazine you want to sell to in your niche does not, pitch your stunning photo to them anyway, you never know whether or how they will decide to use it. However, recognize that a pretty picture is usually not enough. Note how such photos published in other magazines tell a story, either because they include action, or because they are deeply rooted in the niche subject matter. A pretty sunset photo, even if shot from your boat, is not likely to be enough. Your photo must include some element that most readers have not seen before—that is what will grab their attention.

About a Voyage When writing about the voyage you completed (endured?) to reach a place, drama is key. Editors publish these stories because they include all the elements of good fiction: characterization, desire, obstacles, tension, climax, and resolution. If you enjoy a lovely trade winds sail for 25 days, you do not have this type of story (but you may have another type; I will use this example later to illustrate). However, if your mast comes down on day 10, and you sail under jury rig for the next 30 days to reach your destination, anxious about your dwindling water supply, you have a story about a voyage that editors are going to want to buy. And let me add that your voyage does not have to be epic. A near collision on a day sail on the Chesapeake Bay may contain a lesson wrapped in a mini-drama. Nor does your voyage even have to commence. A grave mistake while launching your ski boat that sends your SUV down the ramp and underwater could make a story too (and selling it might offset the insurance deductible). More than most, voyage stories are usually personal, based on direct experience. This is a limiting factor as few of us have many noteworthy voyages to report on. The fount for these story ideas is not gushing, but take from it what you can.

> *The parallel for magazines in other niches: For some magazines, the voyage story is clear, aligning easily with the boating examples I gave. For others, remember that the voyage does not have to be literal. Maybe you are an organic gardener who can write about an internal voyage, a personal journey you took from 1995, when you were a chemist for Monsanto and happened to pick up a copy of* OrganicLife, *to 2015, where you manage a plant nursery and have successfully lobbied your city council to designate four community gardens in your hometown.*

✎ **How-To** This one is self-explanatory. There are two elements to be aware of. First, in The Photos chapter of this book I talk about the nature of the technical photos that accompany How-To stories. Heed this information. Second, this type of story, while easy to write and always in demand by certain magazines (for example, *Good Old Boat* regularly publishes How-To stories), requires a proper tone and perspective to sell. I wrote about this caveat earlier in this chapter, under "Know Your Limitations."

✎ **Book Reviews** This is probably the easiest, least-known way to break into magazine writing. When you factor in the time required to read a book and write the review, the pay is poor. However, if you are reviewing books you want to read anyway, and you are connecting with editors at a magazine you hope to sell longer stories to, the pay suddenly seems like a bonus. Book publishers release more boating-related books each month than busy magazine editors can possibly read and review. Every year, with the increasing popularity of self-publishing, this becomes even truer (though be aware that not all boating magazines publish book reviews, and not all boating magazines that publish book reviews review self-published books). Read the book reviews in your favorite boating magazine. Get familiar with the length and style. Look through past issues and make sure that at least some of the published reviews are by freelancers (people not listed in the masthead). Then find a book you want to read and pitch a review. (I will note that the book does not have to be a new release, simply a release that the magazine has not yet reviewed, or a classic title you think might be ready to be rediscovered.)

If you get the job, take the initiative and contact the book publisher to request a hi-res (300 ppi) JPEG or PDF of the cover image. When you submit your review, submit it with the cover image. You have just saved the editor the time and hassle of contacting the publisher themselves. Maybe you will become the writer they think of first next time they need a book reviewed. Let them know you are interested.

🖉 **Product Reviews** in my experience, a magazine's editorial staff generally handle reviews of new products. In a way, it is one of the perks of their profession. When a manufacturer sends a set of new foul weather gear to the editorial office, one lucky editor gets to keep it post-review. However, once you become a seasoned, dependable writer with strong editor relationships, you may find yourself in a position to review new products a manufacturer sends you. In the meantime, I know of one good opportunity for freelancers to write product reviews: used stuff. Maybe five years ago you bought the newest Harken widget at the boat show, the one that was supposed to make line handling easier. Did it work? What has been your experience? What are your dock mates saying? An editor might be eager to read that story—but only if it has not already been covered to death, and only if your reporting is not spiteful or angry or expected (your story should be somewhat newsworthy). Also, do not think small. Over the years, I have written five reviews of boats for *Cruising World* magazine, for their Classic Plastic section. Two of these were of boats I owned and sailed. Three were of boats belonging to friends I interviewed. Do check with the editor first, however. Luckily, I checked with a *Good Old Boat* editor before starting the review I wanted to write of the boat I currently sail. "As a policy, we don't publish boat reviews written by owners."

The List This is not necessarily a classic Top 10 list, but could also be the "5 Ways to…" or "3 Examples of…" types of articles. The point is to think of ways to categorize information that comprises a story idea to make it more compelling, informative, and accessible to readers. The List is a proven way to do this—just look at how often magazine cover stories use the List format. Think of this story type as a tool in your arsenal. As I showed in the example above, a story about your sailing trip to Catalina Island is not noteworthy and is unlikely to arouse any editor's interest, but if you can write, "Top 5 Attractions for Sailors on Catalina Island," now you have something. When I came up with a story idea for answering the question of how we broke free of conventional life to go cruising as a family with young kids, I could have pitched it as a story of us, of the approach we took. I do not think it would have sold. However, by framing it as "Five Families and How Each Broke Free," I had a much more marketable story to pitch. By adopting the List story type, I also broadened the scope of my story. By including those additional perspectives, I both gave my story more credibility and made it more interesting. Think about all these aspects of this story type as you come up with an idea—then determine the angle (story type) that works best for your idea.

Technical/Informative These are tricky, mostly for the reasons I give below in the section titled Know Your Limitations.

Bottom line, magazines focused on a niche topic really want experts on that topic to write the technical/informative stories; it is how they maintain credibility. If you are a recognized expert, you are golden. If you are not, I write below about how you can overcome this roadblock.

News Shorts Every boating magazine I am aware of features short newsy bits somewhere in the front of the book. In many cases, this content is editor-produced, but if you get a scoop, share it, quick! Fire off a query. Relevant photos will be in demand, especially if the event is happening in a remote location that you happen to be. These pieces will not pay large sums, but measured by the word, short pieces like this often pay very well. Though be aware that for news alerts especially, some editors at smaller pubs do not pay contributors, they simply thank them. Regardless, it is another opportunity to get your byline out there and to build rapport with an editor.

Personal Experience These are voice-of-experience kinds of columns. If you have a story idea that fits this mold, do not limit your pitch to a magazine that has a dedicated column for this story type (though those are excellent choices and allow you to read back issues to study length and writing style). This is a good, reliably saleable framework for a story and you should be able to use it just about anywhere. The downside of this story type is that it is always first person, so your ideas are limited by the number of big lessons you are learning the hard way. I hope that you do not have too many.

Reflection I think many writers out there are more comfortable writing reflection stories than just about any other. This is your chance to frame a unique thought or perspective about your special interest into a story you want to share. Most often, these are heartwarming—grandfather reflecting on a first sail with a grandson—but do not limit yourself. I think it is always refreshing to see a humorous reflection story done right and an editor is likely to give extra points for that. Look at what editors are publishing in your favorite magazine and then start reflecting.

✎ **History Piece** Maybe you want to write about the history of the outboard motor. Maybe you just inherited a 75-year-old Evinrude and want to write about its interesting past. Maybe, while watching *Jeopardy!,* you learned we're coming up on the 100th anniversary of the invention of the outboard motor, and you want to research and write about the inventor. Any of these story ideas are central to the boating niche and saleable to the right magazine. If you enjoy researching and reporting, this is a story idea vein worth tapping.

However, with regard to the anniversary example, know that editors are keen on these types of dates, perhaps anticipating them long before the idea occurs to you. It's their business. However, the only way to find out is to pitch.

Know Your Limitations

I once got an idea for a story on night vision. I wanted to learn and then explain about how the eyes work and the steps a sailor could take, beyond red lighting, to keep or improve their night vision. I spent many hours studying night vision to make sure I had enough material to write such a story. Then I pitched it. Three different editors passed on my idea.

Later I stumbled on information about sacrificial anodes (commonly called zincs because they are an alloy comprised mostly of zinc). I learned about the merits of aluminum-based sacrificial anodes, that aluminum is more effective than zinc in this role because it is lower on the nobility scale. I learned too that unlike aluminum anodes, zinc anodes are made from an alloy that includes cadmium—an awful element from an environmental standpoint. I thought I could write a terrific article based on this info, and with an environmental angle. I pitched it to an editor to whom I had recently sold stories. The response? No thanks.

However, in both cases, I was fortunate to learn why the editor rejected my story idea. Remember that the editor is a wholesaler of your work. He is making your writing a part of a product he is selling to a readership. For your story to be a part of that product, it needs to be well written and you need to be a credible writer. In the case of both my unsold story ideas, the respective editors knew their readers did not want to learn about night vision and sacrificial anodes from the likes of Michael Robertson, an English major who happens to own a boat. Readers expect technical advice and information to come from writers with credentials—perhaps a technician at one of the night vision goggle manufacturers could educate them about night vision. They expect a boating expert with a reputation—perhaps an Ed Sherman, Nigel Calder, or Steve D'Antonio—to tell them what is what with regard to zincs.

I had learned enough about the subject to write a good, informative, accurate article, but that was not enough.

In each case, I had learned enough to write a good, informative, accurate article, but that was not enough. I was not the person to write those articles, not for a magazine that wants to remain an authority.

Write It Like a Reporter

That said, a capable writer without scientific or technical knowledge should be able to sell a particular scientific or technical story so long as two conditions are met.

1. The writer has to take themselves out of the story—in the same way a reporter would—and cite experts in the field.

2. The story has to be one that an expert already writing for the magazine is unlikely to write.

These are difficult conditions to meet. I met them once. I sold a technical story with a more obscure subject to *Ocean Navigator* magazine. It was about why the Southern Ocean is or is not officially considered an ocean (it is not, not like the Atlantic, Pacific, Indian, and Arctic Oceans, but it is a de facto ocean recognized by most scientists, journalists, and countries). I kept myself out of the technical part of the story, instead citing authorities at National Geographic and the International Hydrographic Organization, among others, and wrote the story as a reporter would.

When You Are the Expert

There are cases in which you, the layperson, are the perfect writer to produce and sell a technical story, without removing yourself from it. Boating author Don Casey is much more qualified to write about replacing a hatch on an aging cruising boat, but only you are the expert on your own experience replacing the hatch on your own boat. You cannot offer Casey's expertise, but you can offer something Casey cannot, something that is appealing to readers: your perspective. If you write it right, readers will come away from your story thinking, "Hey, he's a guy just like me and he did it."

Do not ignore the advantage of your lay perspective, leverage it.

Editors know this too, and they will buy this kind of story if it is pitched and written as such. Do not ignore the advantage of your lay perspective, leverage it. Share your trepidation at tackling the project and the mistakes you made and learned from. Highlight those aspects of your story when you write your query. Do not try to write it as if you are hatch replacement expert Don Casey. Know your limitations, and your strengths.

The Magazine

The smallest niche markets may be comprised of only one or two magazines. For these markets, deciding where to send your story may not be such a challenge. However, a larger niche market, such as the boating magazine market, may be comprised of dozens of magazines and a writer must determine which one to pitch. Alternatively, maybe you will come up with ideas for stories that could fit in a boating magazine, but also work in a non-boating magazine.

Imagine, for example, that your story ideas revolve around your boating interest, and your boating interest concerns your 22-foot ski boat that you enjoy trailering to Lake Havasu with the family several times a year. Without even imagining a specific, hypothetical story idea, it is possible to come up with a list of magazines you might end up pitching. The key is to think beyond your specific topic, to include tangential topics and geography. Off the top of my head, I came up with the following list of potential magazine markets.

LAKE/RECREATION
TRAILER BOATING
WATERSKIING
FAMILY VACATIONING
ARIZONA

Using that list, I found online the following magazines that may be good places to pitch your stories (there are undoubtedly more).

ALLIANCE WAKE
ARIZONA HIGHWAYS
ARIZONA KEY
ARIZONA PARENTING (ONLINE)
AZ OUTDOOR
BOATING
(LIST CONTINUES ON FOLLOWING PAGE)

BOATING WORLD
BOATU.S. MAGAZINE
FAMILYFUN
UNLEASHED
WAKE JOURNAL (ONLINE)
WAKEBOARDING
WATERSKI

Once you have a concrete story idea, the next step is to evaluate each magazine for suitability. Is any one of them more likely to publish a story like the one you are writing? For those titles you read regularly, this determination is easy to make. For those you are not familiar with, start by reviewing each magazine's website (perhaps they post online articles from past issues you can read, or perhaps the submission guidelines include content descriptions). Another approach is to visit your local library. If they subscribe to a magazine (or another branch in their system subscribes), they will have at least several back issues available for you to review.

Perhaps your boating interest is more broad, such as the world of sailing. Your interests run the gamut: you crew regularly in the Wednesday night races, you charter annually in the Caribbean, you are planning to go cruising, and you just built a dinghy in your garage. You subscribe to one magazine that publishes content similar to the story you want to write, but you can think of others in which your story might be an even better fit, you just aren't so familiar with them.

Do your due diligence and familiarize yourself with the magazines you want to pitch (never pitch a story to a magazine with which you are not familiar). Following are some of the things to consider when evaluating a magazine as a potential publisher of your story.

   ✎ **What do the title and cover reveal?** You *can* judge a magazine by its cover. Covers are always an extension of the content within. Take *Cruising World* as an example. The title makes it clear it is a cruising-oriented magazine that is not regional. Logically, you might consider *Cruising World* as a place to pitch your story about the magnificent summer you spent exploring the Canadian Gulf Islands aboard a chartered trawler. Then you notice that the covers feature only sailboats. Strike one.

Of course, the magazine next to it, *SAIL*, is out of the question. Yet *Pacific Yachting* might be a perfect fit: the cover text refers to feature destination stories and looking through the stack of back issues, some covers feature sailboats, others powerboats. This might be the right magazine to pitch that story.

✒ **What does the magazine say about itself?** Check out the websites of the magazines you might want to pitch. Sometimes on the About Us page, or more commonly on the Writer's Guidelines page, Submissions page, or Contributor's page, a magazine will be very clear about who they are and the kinds of content they feature. Like many magazines, the *Good Old Boat* website offers writer's guidelines that are very clear about what the editors are looking for from freelance writers:

> *Our niche is cruising sailboats from the 1950s, '60s, '70s, '80s, '90s and 2000s and beyond. We publish articles focused on pride of ownership and articles that discuss upgrades, maintenance, refits, and restoration of good old boats. In addition to these core themes, we publish articles about vendors of good old boat products and services and histories of sailing industry companies and individuals who have influenced the industry. Because these themes are well covered by other magazines, we do not publish:*
>
> - *Destination articles*
> - *Cruising logs*
> - *Racing coverage*
>
> *In addition to technical articles, we also welcome articles focused on sailors and their boats, reflections columns, cruising memories, and other features.*

In just about 100 words, you have learned about the kinds of articles that appear between the covers of *Good Old Boat* and the kinds of stories they specifically do not want.

🖋 **Does the magazine feature content similar to my story or can I imagine my story in this magazine?** The surest way to determine whether a particular magazine is right for your story is to thumb through several issues and get to know it. Find the page or section in the magazine where your story and pictures would go. How would your story fit in there, in the context of the other articles? You need to be able to imagine a place for your story. *BoatU.S. Magazine* might be keen to buy your survey of safe practices for launching a trailerable ski boat, but it is impossible to imagine that same article between the covers of *Latitude 38*. *Ocean Navigator* might be interested in your perspectives after cruising 25,000 miles with an AIS transponder aboard, but that same story is way out of scope for *Good Old Boat*. *Pacific Yachting* will be interested in your survey of the best dockside pubs in the Gulf and San Juan Islands, but *SAIL* will only be interested in a more general story about cruising the same waters (which is a good example of how you can draw two stories from the same experience and sell them both!).

🖋 **Who are the advertisers?** Thumbing through pages, advertisers are another clue to a magazine's content. For example, *Cruising World*, SAIL, and *Blue Water Sailing* are filled with advertisements from sailboat charter companies. If you just finished a two-week sailboat charter in Greece and you are excited to write about it, any of these magazines would be a good place to pitch. Accordingly, you will never find a charter company advertising in *Practical Boat Owner* or *Ocean Navigator* and it would be a waste of time to pitch your charter-focused story to an editor at either of these magazines.

✎ **What is their editorial geography?** *Chesapeake Bay Magazine* makes it clear from their title what their geographic focus is. This is backed up in their writer's guidelines:

> *Chesapeake Bay Magazine is a regional boating publication for those who enjoy reading about the Chesapeake Bay and its tributaries. Appropriate subjects include powerboating, sailing and fishing on the Chesapeake Bay; people, places and history of the Chesapeake region; and the natural history of the Bay.*

You might have a great story from this area that might be a great fit in *SAIL* magazine and others, but *Chesapeake Bay Magazine* might be the place to pitch first, especially if you plan to include lots of local color in your story. Along those lines, you might write the same story a bit differently for *Chesapeake Bay Magazine* vs. *SAIL,* because the former magazine's readership will approach your story with a knowledge of the area you cannot assume for the *SAIL* audience.

✎ **Is it a membership magazine?** From the Aircraft Owners and Pilots Association (AOPA) to the Zoological Society of Milwaukee (ZSM), there are thousands of membership organizations that publish their own magazines. Sometimes these are the most widely circulated magazines covering a particular niche. The America Association of Retired People's (AARP) membership magazine has the largest circulation of any magazine in the world (over 20,000,000). The National Rifle Association publishes several widely circulated magazines available to members. In my boating niche, *BoatU.S. Magazine* (published by

Boat Owners Association of the United States [BOATUS]) circulates twice as many copies as any other boating magazine (over 500,000).

Why does membership matter? Because these pubs are often written for niches within niches. This means that the content they are interested in is very well defined. Take BOATUS. This organization offers boat insurance products and nationwide boat towing services. If I had had a harrowing experience on my trip to Catalina Island that was resolved by a BOATUS tow, *BoatU.S. Magazine* would be the first place (only place) I would turn to pitch my story.

Sometimes it does not matter how well you know however many magazines in the respective market. I once came up with an idea for a story unlike anything I had ever seen in any of them, yet I knew that as a reader I would appreciate it. It was a humorous piece, tongue-in-cheek advice to landlubbers about how to best prepare themselves to host a visiting cruiser in their home.

Of course, it would work only in a magazine whose readership understood cruisers. That narrowed the field considerably. Yet, how did I choose from the cruiser-oriented titles like *Cruising World*, *Yachting Monthly*, *SAIL*, *Cruising Outpost*, and *Blue Water Sailing*?

Know Your Editor

Fortunately, I did not have a sense of just the magazines and their readers, I also had a sense of the editors who work at various magazines. I had never worked with *SAIL* editor Charles Doane, but I had long followed his blog, *Wavetrain*. From his writing there I knew that Charles Doane has a wicked sense of humor. I sent him the following query.

> *Hi Charles,*
>
> *You're the only sailing magazine editor whom I know appreciates humor (I read Wavetrain).*

I wrote the attached 621-word piece on spec. I'm running it by
you first in hopes it has a place in SAIL.

Michael Robertson

Short and sweet. He wrote back to say he liked my story and that
while he isn't the editor who handles such stories, he would forward
it to the editor who does and urge her to publish it. She bought it.

Look Abroad!

When looking for a home for your story—a story that is not geo-
graphically specific—do not forget markets outside of the U.S.

I am a U.S. citizen and I have sold a few articles to foreign magazines, specifically *Pacific Yachting* (Canada) and *Yachting Monthly* (UK).
When you can do it, selling to a foreign publication is a good move.
Not only do foreign magazines serve to enlarge the market you have
to sell to, but oftentimes, they are far enough outside your home market as to not compete, perhaps enabling you to sell the same story
twice.

For English-speaking writers, consider pitching your stories to magazines published outside your home country. If you are a U.S.-based
writer, the foreign markets are comparatively small, but do offer additional opportunities. If you are based outside the U.S., your market
can grow exponentially by pitching outside your home country.

Consider the following numbers for perspective.

The U.S. niche-market magazine, *Boating*, circulates 150,000 copies
per month. In France, that number would put *Boating* in the top 10
magazines in terms of circulation. However, in the massive U.S. magazine market, *Fortune* and *Wired* magazines are near the bottom of the
list of the top 100 magazines—and each circulates more than 850,000
copies per month.

Region-agnostic stories (such as how-to stories) or region-specific
stories (your experience at the Great Barrier Reef for Australia, for
example) may stand the best chance of being published abroad.

Also, when coming up with story ideas for magazines outside your home country, think in terms of leveraging your perspective. For example, there might not be a magazine in Canada interested in a story about your day-to-day experiences dealing with the Canadian health care system before, during, and after your cancer scare. However, that story might be saleable in the U.S. where readers are paying close attention the upheaval of the structure of their own system and may be particularly interested in how things work up north.

Consider the following English-language markets for your stories.

AUSTRALIA
CANADA
IRELAND
NEW ZEALAND
UNITED KINGDOM
UNITED STATES

The single pitfall I have encountered in selling to a foreign publication is being paid with a check drawn from a foreign bank (paid in that country's currency). For each of the stories I sold to *Pacific Yachting*, I received a foreign check. Unfortunately, my U.S. bank would not accept those checks. However, I was in Canada at the time and it was easy to open a Canadian bank account and then cash the checks there. Depending on your bank's foreign check cashing policy, this may not be a problem for you. Additionally, some foreign magazines can pay in dollars. When I sold a feature to Britain's *Yachting Monthly*, they offered to send a check payable in U.S. dollars rather than pounds, which avoided the problem altogether.

The Writing

J ohn Cheever said: "I can't write without a reader. It's precisely like a kiss—you can't do it alone." You may never produce writing on par with Cheever, but if you want to sell your writing, you will do well to write *as* Cheever wrote, with a reader by your side.

The point of inviting the reader to be a part of your writing process is not to crush your creativity or to steer you towards a formulaic approach to writing for a particular audience. Quite the opposite. The point of inviting the reader into your writing room is to make sure they want to stay. You want to remember who they are and to use your writing voice and style and perspective to keep them engaged and by your side.

The moment you get an idea for a story you want to put down on paper, start asking questions about your reader. What is going to pique their interest right at the start and make them want to continue reading your story? What parts of your story are going to be important to them? What assumptions will they make? What knowledge will they bring? What photos are they going to want to see? Answering these questions will help you to write a better story and to take better accompanying photos.

Storytelling is about the communication between writer and reader, teller and listener. If you are not willing to engage a specific readership, your writing will probably not engage a magazine editor—the gatekeeper between you and the readers. Successfully identifying your future reader and then writing for them are critical steps that put you on the path to selling your story. It is that simple, and that difficult.

The Approach

You may have heard or read that in the nonfiction writing world, writers sell their idea for a story or book before they actually write the story or book. This is true, very experienced freelance magazine writers do sell their ideas before writing their stories—some even get paid expenses up front to execute a great idea. Accordingly, books like this one often repeat this approach as advice to unpublished writers looking to become freelance magazine writers. I think this is a mistake. I have a different approach for you, one I often take.

Before I explain what and why, let's look at a successful freelance writer who does sell her ideas before she starts writing.

Diane Selkirk, author of *The Complete Idiot's Guide to Sailing*, has been freelance writing for nearly two decades. She has sold stories to more than 75 different magazines, websites, and newspapers. Diane tells me that after conceiving an idea, she does only the work necessary to draft her query.

> "Different types of stories require different amounts of research in advance of the pitch. For stories based on my personal experience or conceptual pieces, it is easy to go from idea to query and that is all I do. But for others, I'll first hunt down current statistics or other info, maybe develop a list of people I can interview, maybe read a few articles related to the topic—anything I need beforehand to first confirm for me that my idea is viable."

Diane is experienced enough to clearly see the entire path from her idea to her story, without taking a single step. She is able to discern pitfalls that may lie ahead, the information she will need to acquire before embarking, and even whether the journey is feasible.

Of course, the reason Diane and other pros sell their idea before they write their story is so that they do not end up risking time they would spend writing a story they are unable to sell. This approach makes sense for someone with that level of experience.

My advice to you is to go the opposite direction, to risk your time and effort, to risk turning your idea into a story and then never finding an editor who wants to buy it. My advice to you is to consider this risk-laden approach the cost of gaining experience, or the cost of do-ing business. I believe that you—someone getting started writing for the magazines—usually have more to lose by emulating the profes-sional approach. Risk your time! Write at least your first draft before writing your query. I'll tell you why.

Ideas are often difficult to develop into readable stories. Ideas can morph and develop as you turn them into a story. Until you have ex-perience doing this, it can be impossible to see accurately the story embedded in your initial idea.

For example, I recently came up with the idea was to write a feature-length story about the summer we cruised up the Inside Passage, explored Alaska's Glacier Bay, and returned south. Sim-ple enough, but rather than pitch my idea, I started writing. I soon realized that it was impossible to pack all the material I aimed to cover into a single story. Furthermore, through the pro-cess of fleshing out my story I came to learn that the nature of the stories was distinct, demanding two distinct sto-ries. I ended up writing an Inside Pas-sage story and a separate Glacier Bay story—ignoring altogether the return trip south.

> *I believe that you—someone getting started writing for the magazines—usually have more to lose by emulating the professional approach. Risk your time! Write at least your first draft before writing your query.*

Had I pitched my idea as it came to me, before writing those drafts, an editor might have either passed, realizing I was proposing too much scope for a single story, or said yes, only to hear back from me later, apologizing that I could not deliver what I'd promised. Either way, I would have lost.

On several occasions I've come up with ideas I thought would make terrific stories, only to see them crumble and disappear as I tried to flesh them out into a story—those are the ones I'm especially glad I didn't pitch first.

The goal is to get to know your writing self, to become comfortable with your ability to assess ideas. Once you do, you will be able to decide when to pitch an idea for a story you have not begun writing, and when to work through an idea and even flesh out a draft, before pitching.

Another consideration in favor of writing prior to pitching is that even though boating magazines are a niche market in the magazine realm, there are many boating magazines. This is to say there are many places to pitch a story you write on spec. To a lesser or greater extent, this is also the case for other niche markets; there is usually more than one magazine to sell your work to. This means that the actual risk is a bit diffused. If an editor passes on your story idea for reasons beyond your control—such as they've got a similar story on tap for later in the year, or your story isn't a good editorial fit—you'll know that all hope is not lost, you can still pitch that same story to another magazine in the same market.

The goal is to get to know your writing self, to become comfortable with your ability to assess ideas.

Finally, I never pitch very short pieces with a query (nor do I think you should). These I simply write, perfect, and send on spec to an editor (along with a brief note offering the piece). The primary reason for this is that editors are busy. Why make an editor read and respond to your 300-word query for a 150-word piece? In fact, for a story that is only 150 words, I often include the text of the story in the body of the email (in addition to submitting it in an attached, formatted manuscript—helps the editor with contracting and billing).

I learned this lesson by querying a book review for a magazine I knew ran book reviews of about 100 words in length. In my 300-word query, I told the editor how wonderful the book was and why her readers would love it. I ended with an offer to write a review of the book for her magazine.

"You already have," she wrote back. "I'll buy it."

But let me be clear: Except for these very short pieces, I'm advising only that you write your story before you pitch your story idea, not that you submit your manuscript with your query or that you announce to the editor that you've already written the story. The point of writing first is to achieve certainty for yourself that you can write the story you are proposing to sell. Once you know exactly what you have to sell, sell it like a pro.

When it does not make sense to write first

I have sometimes come up with an idea for a story that is a good fit for only a single, specific magazine (perhaps a region-specific story for a specific regional magazine). In those cases especially, I will work like Diane, putting forth just the time and effort I need to feel comfortable writing my query, knowing I can deliver the story I am proposing. Sometimes this means producing a full first draft, but more often, it is simply confirming some facts and lining up interviews ahead of time.

Perhaps the best case for pitching your idea before writing is that you need editorial input before writing. This is not to say that your idea isn't solid—never write a query with an idea you haven't fully developed or cannot articulate—but that you need some editorial parameters. For example, maybe you came up with an idea, considered it thoroughly, began fleshing it out in an outline, and then realized there were more than one very different directions you could take your story. Maybe this is a story you could turn into either a 2,500-word feature or a 500-word piece. Maybe you see it as something in between, but you are not sure where that would fit into the magazine.

Why make an editor read and respond to your 300-word query for a 150-word piece?

Maybe you can see writing your story either as an instructional primer, or as an entertaining and inspiring tale. This is probably a good time to stop and write your query. In this query, you will want to be very clear and specific about your idea, but then solicit the editor's input by offering to deliver one of a couple different stories, the one they prefer.

Edit, Re-write, Repeat

You can increase your likelihood of success by putting forth the effort required to make sure the story you are trying to sell is the best it can be. You have to make sure your sentences are clear—not muddied with too many adverbs and adjectives. You have to make sure your writing is tight—notice that the articles you read in magazines tend to get straight to the point and then they do not divert. Especially if you are writing a feature, you have to ensure that your prose is interesting and pulls the reader along. You have to make sure that your text is error-free. The better and cleaner the copy you submit, the greater the likelihood the editor will buy your story—and the greater the likelihood you will become a writer they want to work with again.

Writing is a skill that can always be honed. I hope that every year you will be able to look back at the work you produced the previous year and clearly see how it could be better. However, do not wait twenty years to become the next Steinbeck before trying to become a published writer. Now is the time. Your voice is unique and if you have opened this book, you have a desire to share it. Start typing.

Do not rely only on yourself to edit and sharpen your writing. Just don't. You are not qualified to do so. I cannot spot all the problems in my own writing; Stephen King cannot spot all the problems in his writing. Writing may be a solitary act, but once you have your first draft complete, enlist the troops. (I am not talking about the spell-check utility that is a part of your word processor.)

Identify the readers, writers, editors, or grammarians in your life who are willing to read your draft and offer critique. The more input you get—especially when you are getting started—the better. In a short time, you should be able to see who it is that gives you the most critical and insightful feedback, the yin to your yang? If you are lucky, this is more than one person and you are able to reciprocate. I rely heavily on my wife, Windy—she is a fantastic editor—but if you can find more than one person to review your manuscripts, all the better. I hope that when you review their feedback, you will be eager to address the flaws in your story and make it better.

Is this the end?

No.

Regardless of the extent of the changes you made to your manuscript in response to the feedback (could range from a light edit to a complete re-write), I think you can help yourself by putting your story aside for a week—a month even—before looking at it with fresh eyes and then again trying to make it better.

Only after you've done all you can to ensure you've got the cleanest, most compelling story you can produce, should you send it to a magazine editor. I cannot overemphasize the importance of these review and re-write steps. I know first-hand how much work and patience they take (do you think for a minute that this book was written in one, two, or even three drafts?). But hopefully—especially if you're reluctantly soliciting outside reviews and believe your first draft is spot-on—you wind up with a final draft that is so improved from your original best try, that you're pleased and humbled and sold on the value of including other people in the review and edit process.

> *Only after you've done all you can to ensure you've got the cleanest, most compelling story you can produce, should you send it to a magazine editor.*

Know that with experience, you will be able to streamline your writing and editing process; you will know intuitively which pieces to invest more time in.

The reward of all this time and effort goes beyond publication and a check. Your writing and your confidence in your writing will improve through the process, every single time. And you know what? That will make you want to write more.

When an Editor is Not an Editor

In case you think otherwise, the niche magazine editor to whom you will sell your story is an *acquiring* editor, not a line editor or a developmental editor or a copyeditor or a proofreader or a writing teacher or a hand holder. She is perfectly qualified to mark-up, hack, and even re-write your prose until it shines, but she probably will not, she likely does not have time (and it's in your best interest to assume she does not). She is likely to reject your on-spec submission if she thinks it needs more than minor tweaks. (Though if she particularly likes your idea, she may give you another chance by asking you to revise extensively or to cut 500 words, for example.)

Despite the power you attribute to them ("If they decide to buy my story, I'll realize my lifelong dream of being published!"), the magazine editor is not a deity. Rather, she is just a hard-working professional whose primary responsibility is to recognize well-written stories that will appeal to her readers, apply minor edits to stories as needed for clarity or space or style considerations, and offer you money. So never expect an edit from the editor, that is all on you.

Things went very differently for a friend, writer Sara Dawn Johnson (www.saradawnjohnson.com), when she sold a feature-length story to the online arm of *The Atlantic* this past year. Over the course of a few drafts, *The Atlantic* editor gave Sara specific input on refining her piece until it shined and fit the tone and style of the publication. Sara's experience highlights the difference between mainstream magazines and niche magazines. The smaller editorial staffs of smaller publications are usually too burdened to give a writer as much attention.

The Photos

Imagine you spent the summer in Alaska's Prince William Sound aboard your sailboat. The things you saw and experienced were incredible and you know just how to relate them in words that paint a picture that will pull a reader out of their own head and put them back aboard with you, ooh-ing and ahh-ing. Alternatively, let's say you can masterfully hook a reader by describing the terror of the day you almost got into a wreck because the brakes on your boat trailer failed on the highway, and then clearly and concisely explain the steps you took to diagnose and repair the problem. In either case—assuming you query the right magazine—you will probably find that editors are eager to print your story.

However, in both cases, suppose you have no pictures to accompany your story. None. No photos of rugged, pristine wilderness, none of the crack in the fitting that allowed the fluid to slowly leak from your master brake cylinder. Your chances of being published just disappeared. You may have the chops to write your story, but words are not enough.

Of course, there are exceptions to the picture rule. I write book reviews that never require an accompanying picture from my camera (only a book cover image

Get proficient with a camera because no niche-market magazine is going to send a photographer out to capture your story. It is all you.

from the publisher). *SAIL* and *Pacific Yachting* have each bought stories from me that their staff illustrated in-house, either because my stories did not lend themselves to photos, or because in-house illustrations fit the magazine's style for the particular column. However, you can count on the sale of any feature story—and nearly everything else—being dependent on there being great pictures to accompany great text. Like it or not, all the very hard work you put into being a writer is not enough. Get proficient with a camera because no niche-market magazine is going to send a photographer out to capture your story. It is all you.

If you are already a confident and experienced photographer, you are far ahead in the game. If you only occasionally snap photos of your family on vacation with a point-and-shoot, it's time to begin applying the same focus to photography as you give to writing. And before you bristle at the thought of another hurdle on the path to selling your writing to the magazines, consider that this need to produce great photos is not an activity that is necessarily separate from the writing job. Often, taking photos to accompany a story is an integral step in developing and shaping your story.

Do not despair if you are not Annie Leibovitz and you do not know the difference between aperture and f-stop.

When we recently traveled through the Marquesas archipelago in the South Pacific, I viewed our experience through my camera viewfinder with an eye on the story I wanted to write. I saw each photo I took (I took a lot) in terms of how it would look in the pages of a magazine, in terms of how it would illustrate the thoughts and emotions I was experiencing. I ended up shooting some of the same images in both vertical and horizontal orientations. I took close-up pictures of hibiscus flowers because I knew one could be used as a colorful, accenting photo to help capture the beauty of the place. I took photographs of Marquesan people in day-to-day settings—not because they were doing anything amazing, but because I knew I might capture a photo that would help readers to understand the setting. Writers refer to this process as creating an image story. It is perhaps equal in importance to your word story.

In the past, when I documented my travels with my camera, nearly all my pictures were personal (me and my family posing) or of pretty landscapes or just plain cliché and uninteresting. Take a critical look at the photos that illustrate a freelancer's feature story in a magazine you would like to sell to. Do they look like the pictures in your photo album?

Do not despair if you are not Annie Leibovitz and you do not know the difference between aperture and f-stop. I don't either. You do not need to be *that* good or know *that* much to sell photos with your stories (at which point you will be able to start calling yourself a professional photographer!). You just need to heed the following.

- ✎ **Pick up a book on basic photography.** Sharpen your skills and learn to take photos that will catch an editor's eye. Pay attention to the sections that teach you, for example, to take photos in the morning or afternoon hours, when the sun is lower and colors are deeper. Learn about light—where you want it to illuminate your subject. Learn about composition and the importance of foreground, middle ground, background, and including people in your pictures. Get to the point where you at least begin to recognize these aspects in the freelance photos your favorite magazine publishes. Pay attention to what you like about the photos you see in the magazines. How could you have captured the same images? Would you have thought to be where the shooter is? Get to the point where you begin thinking of these things when you are out and about, raising that camera to your face. It will make a big difference.

- ✎ **Buy a decent camera(s).** Some photographers can take excellent photos using smartphones or cheap cameras (and occasionally, all of us can). However, you are likely to get more reliable, predictable results with a proper camera. If you are an amateur who is serious about selling your photos to magazines, I think you will benefit from shooting with a decent digital SLR camera with a decent lens (or a very good point-and-shoot camera). Even if you are never capable of using this camera to its full potential, all else being equal, the automatic settings on this camera will often do a good job of making your pictures look better than you deserve. You want every edge you can get when selling your photos to the magazines.

However, that does not mean you should go overboard and spend a fortune. The law of diminishing returns applies and a mid-range digital SLR camera and a stock lens will probably serve you well.

For what it's worth, I currently use a Nikon D90 (with a fast Nikon 35mm prime lens and a Tokina 11-16 wide-angle lens) and augment with a Canon PowerShot Elph 100HS (with Ikelite underwater housing) for underwater shots. My writing friend Behan Gifford (www.sailingtotem.com/) sells the photos she takes with a hand-me-down Nikon D40 and back-up Nikon D5100, both with various lenses. For underwater shots, she uses a Canon PowerShot D20. Author and photographer Pat Schulte (www.bumfuzzle.com) currently uses high-end gear, but he has been at it for a decade and publishes dozens of art-house-quality photos each week online. He carries a Canon 6D full-frame DSLR with a zoom lens, a Canon 50mm prime, and a 15mm wide angle. Additionally, Pat uses a Fujifilm X100T for backup.

Do not leave your camera at home. Keep it handy and shoot with an eye for potential stories. Oftentimes, the ideas you come up with require photos that are impossible to take after-the-fact (like that story on how to re-bed a leaky port light—better hope you still have others to do!).

Polarize. You know those photos of tropical settings that seem set in Technicolor with the varying shades of turquoise water lapping at white sand beaches against a background of deep blue sky and white puffy clouds? I guarantee you the photographer used a polarizing filter on his lens. Just like polarizing sunglasses, these filters cut glare and water reflection and bring out the depths of colors of the outdoors. Especially if boating is your niche, or for anytime you are shooting on or near the water, get a decent polarizing filter for your lens. It may very well make the difference between photos an editor loves, and photos they decline.

✎ **Practice.** Digital photography has made it easier and cheaper than ever to practice taking pictures—you get to see your results right away (too much back lighting!) and there is no film to pay for (delete!). Take advantage of this to experiment, capturing multiple versions of every shot, changing any aspect you can think of. Get down on your belly, stand high on that bench, adjust the camera settings, include people in the picture, exclude people from the picture, shoot portrait, shoot landscape, come back tomorrow when the light is different, play with the polarizing filter.

✎ **Don't be shutter shy.** Take many photos. Then take more. You may delete tons of unwanted photos later, but you may also make a beautiful mistake and capture a magical shot you did not intend, one that helps you sell your story. Absent real talent and proficiency, you have to play the odds. That is how I do it.

✎ **Don't be manipulative.** I never crop, brighten, rotate, or manipulate photos in any way before I submit them to the editors I work with. Magazines employ designers who will do with your photos what they wish. If you straighten the tilted horizon or fix a red eye, you may degrade the image to the point that they may elect not to use it. JPEG files are especially sensitive to degradation this way. That said, if the writer's or photographer's guidelines are not explicit, and you've not worked with a particular magazine before, and you are an experienced photographer,

ask the editor whether he would prefer you pre-process photos you submit.

Two Types of Photos

To sell a range of stories to the magazines, you are going to need to become proficient in taking two types of accompanying photos: technical photos and journalistic photos. (These are my terms, by the way.) Technical photos are those you take to illustrate how-to or technical stories (such as describing the installation of a new cabin hatch). Journalistic photos are those you take to depict adventures or places or people (such as a story about a group of friends crossing the Atlantic Ocean together for the first time).

Technical Photos

For technical stories, such as ones that describe upgrade or repair projects from start to finish, photos have to be precise, sometimes instructional, always clearly illustrating a specific subject or outcome, sometimes with a step-by-step progression. While the photos for technical stories may seem to lack a need for an artistic sensibility, there remains an absolute need for the photographer to consider lighting, composition, and other factors.

Think very narrow focus. People are rarely included in these photos, and then only when appropriate to personalize the project or to add necessary scale. Your husband might be extremely photogenic, but asking him to pose next to the finished doohickey installation your story describes, is not necessarily helpful.

Think like an editor. Consider whether magazine readers who will read your story will prefer to see the largest possible rendering of the installed doohickey, or squint to see it in a photo that includes elements not relevant to the installation. Consider when close-ups and extreme close-ups may be necessary. The best approach for determining how to frame and capture technical photos is to study the photos that accompany similar articles in magazines.

On its website, *Good Old Boat* magazine features an excellent guide for taking technical photos (www.goodoldboat.com/writers _guidelines/photography.php). Composed by Paula Biles of Sea-worthy Goods, this resource for writers contains clear technical photo requirements (such as photo size and file type), instructions for naming and managing photo files, and dozens of examples of photos that work and photos that don't—with clear explanations. In addition, this resource offers the following tips for freelance writers capturing photographs to illustrate technical stories:

- Concentrate on what your article is trying to show or demonstrate. Remove any distractions. Imagine how the photos will clarify your article and explain things difficult to put into words. Visualize how the images will look on the printed page.

- Isolate and simplify your subject. Make certain what you are showing contrasts with the background. If your article is about solving a problem, show the essential steps toward the solution without visual distractions. In a boat review, the boat should be the center of attention. When you are composing the photo, check all four corners for unwanted distractions. It is crucial to remove visual clutter.

- Keep the horizon level and bulkheads upright.

- Think like a camera. It is all about light and contrast. Avoid harsh shadows and bright patches by shooting in muted natural light, when the sky is slightly overcast. This will show details clearly without distracting bright spots or dark obscuring shadows. If photography in bright sun is unavoidable, have someone hold an umbrella or car sunscreen to shade your subject or use their body to block the rays. Sometimes a flash will remove shadows on close subjects and a polarizing filter can help reduce glare and reflections.

In boat interiors, avoid the reflected flare on smooth and varnished surfaces by shooting in soft diffused light.

🖉 Get sharp. Focus should be extremely precise, especially with close-ups. Use a small flexible tripod. If that is not possible, steady the camera on a bag of rice, your first mate's shoulder, or a bulkhead. Use your camera's remote control or timer to get a steadier shot. For point-and-shoot cameras, check your focus settings.

🖉 Use creative perspectives. Try a variety of heights, angles, and distances from the subject. Experiment with different zoom distances, using the camera and your feet. Slight changes can make a big difference in emphasis, lighting, and background clutter. Try a waterproof camera to shoot at or below the waterline.

🖉 Leave breathing space around the main image for the graphic designer to work with.

🖉 Persistence and the delete key are essential for getting good (and great) photos. The better the photographers, the more photos they take…and delete.

Journalistic Photos

Journalistic photos are entirely different. For these, your primary goal is eye-catching color, drama, or beauty. Editors want photos that grab their attention, regardless of whether the photo makes them long to be where you were, or glad they are not.

In nearly all cases, journalistic photos benefit from the inclusion of people.

A photo of the inside of a boat's cabin following a knockdown at sea will grab an editor's (and reader's) attention and illustrate a dramatic tale (and not leave anyone wishing they were there). That is an effective photo. Conversely, a photo of smiling friends relaxing in the cockpit of a boat at anchor in the tropics with a blazing sun setting behind them will make anyone wish they were there. That is also an effective photo.

In nearly all cases, journalistic photos benefit from the inclusion of people. In the example of the cabin in disarray post-knockdown, the writer could dramatically improve that photo by showing the human side of the drama. Put the chaos in the background and focus on the despair and resignation on the face of the photographer (selfie!). Or perhaps capture a crewmember, ankle-deep in water, headlamp on, sorting through the mess. Minus the people, the cockpit photo example could be a gorgeous sunset picture in the tropics. However, the smiling friends—engaged with each other—allow the reader to imagine themselves in the scene, with the people, as content as they obviously are. Neither picture is as powerful without the human element.

I just read an article in *Cruising World* magazine by long-time contributor Webb Chiles. He tells a tale of a tough, solo, Pacific Ocean passage. It is a feature story that includes four photos he took. Despite having sailed alone, Chiles appears in three of them. The picture he does not appear in is one that shows the bleakness of the stormy ocean. Looking at the other

> *"So when you are out taking pictures, by all means keep an eye out for the amazing, but do not let the magic of the ordinary pass you by."*

pictures, they would not be nearly as effective if Chiles had not set the timer and included himself in the frames. We need to see him out there, doing what he is describing in the story. Chiles knows this. That is why he took care to photograph himself, to include a humanizing element. (That is why he is a long-time contributor to the magazine.)

Ever notice how television and film actors do not look at the camera? The people in your photos do not have to avoid the camera as studiously, but it is often (not always) better if they do. In the case of the earlier knockdown photo example, I suggested that a face shot, either the photographer or crewmember staring into the camera, might offer a desired effect, allowing the reader to study the projected emotions. However, in the friends-socializing-in-the-cockpit photo, imagine how different two photos could be. In one, four friends are posed, arms around each other, all smiling and focused on the camera. In the other, the same four are equally happy, but one is in the middle of speaking, mouth partially open, hands gesturing, the three others focused on him, laughing or smiling at what he is saying. The second photo tells a story and paints a much more interesting scene for the reader to absorb. You want that shot.

Shoot the Ordinary

For years, author and photographer Pat Schulte has captured the moods and beauty of streetscapes around the world. He does it very well (www.bumfuzzle.com). I asked him for advice on photographing a place to best illustrate a story.

> "I avoid the tendency to photograph only the extraordinary. Often, what's really worth taking photos of is the ordinary: the fruit seller, the row of identical cars, the crying baby sitting in the center of the plaza. This is especially true when shooting in a place geographically removed from your audience. Life goes on very much the same everywhere, but with dramatic differences that you should seek to capture with your camera. My readers already know what it looks like to go to the store to buy eggs, but have they ever seen someone buying eggs from the back of a pickup truck, where the chickens are for sale too? They've bought tacos a hundred times from

their local fast-food joint, but have they ever stood in front of a food cart and had them made fresh with hot tortillas and scorching salsas? City streets are a favorite of mine. Where I'm from in the U.S., cities are all blacks and grays. But take a picture on a typical street in Guanajuato, Mexico, or Valparaiso, Chile, or San Juan, Puerto Rico, and you'll be hard pressed to find a dull color. So when you're out taking pictures, by all means keep an eye out for the amazing, but don't let the magic of the ordinary pass you by."

Getting Technical: Pixels and Files

Before smartphone cameras got so good that many consumers stopped buying cameras and paying attention to camera development, there was a lot of press about the ever-increasing number of pixels that camera manufacturers advertised for new models. Specifically, critics reported how these numbers are largely insignificant to users who will never reproduce their photos in print sizes large enough to warrant the kind of resolution promised by 12 megapixel images. I mostly agree…however, for you, amateur photographer hoping to capture images that an editor will want to print in their magazine, higher pixel counts can work for you. Here is why.

In general, magazines will not print images with a resolution under 300 pixels per inch (ppi). That is an easy rule to remember, but what does it mean? Let us first define the pixel.

A pixel is the basic unit of a digital image. Each pixel represents a tiny portion of the surface area of an image. All of the pixels that comprise an image are of equal—not static—size.

So consider an image measuring 4-inches by 6-inches. If the resolution of that image is 100 ppi, it means that there are 100 pixels in each linear inch. You can say the dimensions of the photo are 400 by 600 pixels. You can say that the total number of pixels comprising the image is 240,000. All correct.

This 400-by-600-pixel image may look okay on your computer monitor, but it does not contain enough pixels to appear sharp when printed at that size (as in a magazine).

Note that while the total number of pixels used to comprise an image is fixed and unchanging, the ppi is variable, dependent on the physical size the image is displayed or printed. In this case, if we reduce the physical size of the image, from 4x6 inches to 1x1.5 inches, the ppi value changes from 100 ppi to 400 ppi. (Right? Because remember that this will always be a 400x600-pixel image—240,000 total pixels.) This is sharp enough for printing, but probably too small for an editor to want to feature. If we go the other way and increase the physical size of the image, to 6x9 inches, we are down to about 66 ppi. This is because each of the same 240,000 pixels had to increase in size to cover a larger area. When pixels increase in size, you see them. This image will definitely appear grainy (pixelated).

In general, magazines will not print images of a resolution under 300 pixels per inch (ppi).

Okay, so 300 ppi is the threshold you do not want to go below, and you understand what 300 ppi means. However, how do you know if your photos are 300 ppi or larger, and why is it a good idea to exceed this number?

Once you have uploaded your photos to your computer, it is easy to see the size of the image in terms of pixels. However, remember that ppi is variable, depending on the physical size that the magazine's art director decides to print your photo. Because you cannot know the physical size the art director will want to print your photo, it makes sense to calculate the pixel dimensions of a large photo, say 8x10 inches at 300 ppi. Of course, this is 2400x3000 pixels.

Now, find the file for a photo on your computer—one that you have uploaded from your camera and is otherwise untouched.

🖉 If you are on a PC...

Right-click the file name. On the submenu that displays, select Properties. The system will display the Properties dialog box, with the General tab displayed by default (ignore the Size and Size on Disk information displayed on this tab). Click the Details tab. Scroll down to the Image heading and note the listed Dimensions. This value is in pixels—it is the info you are looking for (ignore the Horizontal Resolution and Vertical Resolution values reflected in dpi, they are irrelevant to you).

🖉 If you are on a Mac...

Right-click the file name. On the submenu that displays, select Get Info. The system will display the Info panel. In the first General pane, the system lists file information. Beneath this, in the More Info pane, you will find the image dimensions you are looking for. Many Mac users also simply open the image file in the Preview app as that system displays the image dimension info there too.

> *It is worth noting too, that both the PC and Mac can be configured to display image dimensions (in pixels) with the file name (in one of the Details view columns on a PC, beneath the name, in blue font, on the Mac).*

Okay, so you have the image dimensions in pixels, the image size your camera is currently shooting. Is it greater than or about the same as the 2400x3000 pixels we calculated would be necessary to print an image at 8x10 inches at 300 ppi? Anything at or close to this size is probably adequate.

However, I also wrote more is better. I wrote this even considering the extra hassle that large file sizes require, in terms of sharing. Let me tell you why this is true.

Imagine you take an amazing photo, one that the magazine may want to spread out over one-and-a-half pages at the start of your article. Fortunately, you had configured your camera to produce large images, 3000x4500 pixels. The art director could almost spread your magnificent shot across two pages. All is right in the world, or is it?

The problem is that unless you framed that photo ideally, the art director is going to want to crop your photo, maybe extensively. This means stripping away portions of your image (pixels). The editor or designer will then have to enlarge the image to fill the page. Are there enough pixels remaining to achieve the desired sharpness? I hope that there are (sometimes larger photos can get away with slightly lower ppi values).

So shoot pictures with larger image sizes. It can only make your photos more attractive to the magazines. Tanya Loranca, the art designer for *Cruising World* magazine, echoes the point. "There have been times I've had to enlarge a 300 ppi picture to fit a space, to the point where the resolution dipped below 300. If the image is really clear then it will work, but if the image is not, I may decide to not use it."

Therefore, for a professional writer who needs professional-quality photos to sell with their words, cameras capable of higher resolutions can be a real asset. But only if you always shoot at a high-resolution setting (get a bigger storage chip if larger file sizes are a problem).

JPEG or JPG?

These format names and file extensions are synonymous. In both cases, they refer to the Joint Photographic Experts Group, the organization that created this popular image format. A long time ago, early versions of Windows would not accept the four-letter file extension (.jpeg) and so it was shortened (.jpg). This restriction is gone, but the three- and four-letter format names and file extensions both remain and can be used interchangeably.

Camera makers still tout the numbers of megapixels their cameras can shoot. A megapixel is about 1 million pixels (exactly 1,048,576). Therefore, an 8-megapixel camera can shoot an image that contains roughly 8 million pixels. The big image I referenced above, 3000x4500 pixels, contains about 13.5 million pixels.

However, neither do megapixels tell the whole story. Some smartphones now boast cameras that shoot 13 megapixels. Nevertheless, their lenses and sensors are small compared to a digital SLR that shoots 8 megapixels. This means they are working with comparatively less light to produce an image—and light is everything. In most cases, I would wager the DSLR would produce an image with the qualities more likely to attract an editor and art director than the smartphone.

> ### PPI vs. DPI?
>
> *PPI means pixels per inch. Pixels are the unit used when measuring the resolution of digital photos. (Interestingly, I read that pixel is a word that originated from two words: picture element.) Though people often use the two acronyms interchangeably, this is incorrect. DPI means dots per inch. Dots and DPI are printer terms and should be used only in that context.*

When it comes to file types, Tanya welcomes either RAW or JPEG files. In my experience, this is common, but do check the submission guidelines for the specific magazine to which you intend to submit.

If you are writing a story about a time before the digital age and the only photos you have are the ones in your photo album, you are not out of luck. In my experience, the editor will ask you send in the original negatives so the magazine can scan them. If you do not have these, he will likely want you to send in the original photos so they can scan those.

The Query & Pitch

The query you write to pitch your story is a marketing tool. Without being verbose, you want to sell your idea for a story to an editor. I believe the best way to do this is to clearly describe the idea so that it can sell itself.

The first thing you want to do before drafting a query to an editor at a magazine you've not pitched before, is to check out the magazine's writer's guidelines, if they're made available. They are occasionally printed in a magazine, near the masthead. However, more often, your best bet is to go online, to the magazine's website. Yet, because magazines structure their websites for readers, information intended for writers is usually buried and may be difficult to find (scan the links at the bottom of the page, or check the About Us or Contact page). What you are looking for may be called Writer's Guidelines, but I have also seen them listed as Submission Guidelines, or Submissions, or Contributors, or Writers and Photographers. If there are none, at the very least you should find contact information for the editorial department.

However, no matter how comfortable your business relationship becomes, never stop working to grab the editor's attention.

If there are writer's guidelines, pay attention to any explicit instructions and follow them. Consider it a test. Often, these guidelines include a lot of information that will be useful to you (the kinds of stories they publish, the fees they pay, the email address to use for sending queries), but no information about how to write a proper, effective query.

The bottom line is that your query should grab the editor's attention and it should be succinct. Resist adding any superfluous information, such as, "I know my idea for a story will work because I've already developed it into a terrific first draft." Those are 19 superfluous words.

In the absence of any specific query guidelines from the magazine, you should write a query that includes the following six elements (and probably nothing more). Consider using the following as a checklist:

1. **A name.** Have a specific person in mind and spell their name correctly. (Later in this chapter, in the section, "Pitching the Query," I give instructions for determining the specific person to whom you should address your query and send your pitch.) I encourage you not to open with "Dear" and to use the person's full name without any Mr./Ms. titles. (What if you got it wrong?!) Once you have corresponded with an editor, consider addressing further correspondence and future queries using just the editor's first name—follow their lead as you would for any business correspondence.

2. **A hook.** Be sure your opening sentence(s) is likely to spark an editor's interest and relate to your story. Even if the subject of your story is as dry as Death Valley—such as replacing the wood hatches on a 1970s cruising boat—the least you can do is to make it sound interesting. It is your job. After all, if you are expecting an editor to buy your story based only on your short description, it should be a very good short description. You do not want an editor thinking, "If they aren't hooking me with their query, will they hook my readers with their story?" Consider this opening to a query for the aforementioned hatch replacement story, "The crack of splitting wood isn't one of the normal sounds our boat makes when tacking. I learned it's the sound of an old wood deck hatch being ripped apart by a windward jib sheet."

3. **An offer.** Immediately after your hook, cut to the chase. Tell the editor what you have to sell. "I would like to offer you a 1,000- to 1,500-word story about the steps I took to remove and replace the original wood hatches on my 1978 Fuji 40. I

will write about the challenges I faced sourcing well-made and reasonably-priced modern replacement hatches, and about how I fit them to both improve aesthetics and lower the risk of future damage from sheet entanglement." By the way, note the standard industry language, "I'd like to offer you..." It may sound to you like you are giving your story away to an editor for free. You aren't. They know you want money. Just use this language.

4. **A picture (or two, or more).** Let the editor know you are prepared to provide the pictures they will need to illustrate your story and turn it into an attractive article. Of course, there is no need to say that. Here is how I address it in my example: "I have excellent pictures that document every step of the project, all of them in good outdoor light and from multiple perspectives."

5. **Bona fides.** Have you been published before? If not, ignore this step. If you have been, even if in your school paper or a magazine unrelated to boating, let the editor know. However, if your clippings exceed a half-dozen, pick the most impressive or most relevant six and do not list any more than that. "My words and pictures have been published in several boating magazines over the years, this past year in *Cruising World*, *Good Old Boat*, *Pacific Yachting*, *SAIL*, and *Yachting Monthly*."

6. **A closing.** Remember that the editor gets many queries from lots of writers. The editor must read them all, looking for jewels (like yours!). If you are grateful for their time and consideration, say so. Then tell them that you look forward to hearing from them (because you do, right?). "I appreciate your time and consideration and I look forward to hearing from you." Then simply sign off with a "Sincerely" (not "Warmly" or "Fondly" or "Your friend"—this is a business letter).

What you should end up with is something like the following, clear and concise:

> *Karen Larson,*
>
> *The crack of splitting wood is not one of the normal sounds our boat makes when tacking. I learned it is the sound of an old, wood deck hatch being ripped apart by a windward jib sheet.*
>
> *I would like to offer you a 1,000- to 1,500-word story illustrating the steps I took to remove and replace the original wood hatches on my 1978 Fuji 40. I will write about the challenges I faced sourcing well-made and reasonably priced modern replacement hatches, and about how I fit them to both improve aesthetics and lower the risk of future damage from sheet entanglement.*
>
> *I took excellent pictures that document every step of the project, all of them in good outdoor light and from multiple perspectives.*
>
> *My words and pictures have been published in several boating magazines over the years, this past year in Cruising World, Good Old Boat, Pacific Yachting, SAIL, and Yachting Monthly.*
>
> *I appreciate your time and consideration and I look forward to hearing from you.*
>
> *Sincerely,*
>
> *Michael Robertson*

I do not mind getting a rejection from an editor whom I believe completely understood what I was proposing. He may have a similar story scheduled for a future issue. The worst thing is being able to discern from a rejection letter (if you are fortunate enough to get one) that the editor misunderstood your story idea. At that point, it is game over. You cannot send a follow-up email that says, "I apologize, I don't think I was clear and I think you misunderstood my query. What

I meant was…" No. Your job as a writer is to be clear and to be understood. Fix it and query the next magazine editor on your list.

Once you build a relationship with an editor, your queries can be a little less formal. However, no matter how comfortable your business relationship becomes, never stop working to grab the editor's attention. You will need to do it in the story anyway, for the reader, so you might as well preview your winning hooks in your query letters.

To be successful, you should communicate professionally, remaining cognizant of the needs and wants of the people to whom you wish to sell your product.

Finally, be up front! If your story or any part of it was published before, whether on your blog or in a local newspaper or in another magazine, share this information with the editor at the time you pitch your story. In many cases, unless the distribution of your story was wide and recent, pre-publication will not be a limiting factor.

Communication Tips

Writing may be your art, your craft, your passion, or your hobby, but to sell it, you must remember that for the editors with whom you are corresponding, your writing is an element of their business, their career, their profession. To be successful, you should communicate professionally, remaining cognizant of the needs and wants of the people to whom you wish to sell your product.

The first time I sent a query to a magazine editor, it was like a cold call. I was trying to sell an idea to someone who did not know me from Adam, and I did not know her. This was difficult, but once I sold that story and exchanged several emails with that editor about that story, subsequent pitches to that editor were simpler to write and less formal. Additionally, perhaps because my confidence increased, pitches to other editors at other magazines were easier to write.

Like every business in the print publishing world, magazines are under tremendous financial pressures. Accordingly, fewer people are doing the same work in 2016 than were in 2006. Editors are generally over-worked. Keep this in mind when writing your query or communicating with a magazine editor and you will improve your chances of selling a story. Following are some recommendations.

✎ Do not oversell yourself. There is no shame in pitching your first story idea. You want to show that you took the time to understand the business by writing a clean, compelling query, but you do not want to try to make it seem like you have more writing experience than you do. Trying to inflate your credentials makes you look silly, and diminishes your chances of selling your story.

✎ Do not pitch on paper. This is the information technology age. An editor's workflow is on their computer. You may think you will stand out; you will only make the editor's job more difficult.

✎ Keep email correspondence short and direct. Say what you have to say as clearly and concisely as possible. Do not send an email that forces an editor to decipher its meaning. Do not send an email with a bunch of superfluous words or messages that the editor has to wade through to get to your question(s). Following is a good example of how your communications might read (with an editor with whom you've been corresponding):

Hi Tim,

I got your email and I have a couple questions.

1. What kind of a word count are you looking for?

2. I have a two-week vacation coming up; can I deliver this by June 15?

Thank you,

Michael Robertson

At the same time, one of your goals as a writer should be to develop a rapport with the editors with whom you correspond. Being human helps assure an editor that your writing will be lively and approachable. According to writer Diane Selkirk, "Being an individual helps your pitch stand out from all the robotic pitches that land in an editor's inbox each month." But do not try to develop a rapport by sending chatty, personal emails or sending a Facebook Friend request. Your shortest (and only) path to a good rapport is by being responsive, courteous, and professional. Down the road, once you have that rapport, you may decide to communicate more personally (thereby exposing your wit or magnetic personality). In fact, down the road this rapport can work for you. Diane recently emailed a brief question to an editor about a story she was working on. Before signing off, she added that her family was in Madagascar and that she had spent the morning watching locals re-rig a traditional sailing dhow. The editor got back to her quickly with an answer to her question and a suggestion that she pitch a story on sailing dhows.

✐ Don't get impatient. Time will come to a stop for you while you wait for an editor to get back to you about a query or submission. Deal with it. Start writing the next story and put this one out of your mind. Do not follow up until at least a month has passed. The process can be frustratingly slow, but that is the nature of the beast. Editors work on issues months in advance and some structure their workload so that they read and respond to unsolicited queries only once a month. It is not the squeaky wheel whose stories are purchased.

✐ Follow a proper format for writing your query and pitching your story. Do not try to get cute with your story pitch so that you stand out from the pack. Do not use a purple comic sans font. Do not use emoticons. Do not attach a video clip of your kids on your boat saying hello to the editor by name and holding a handmade sign with the name of the magazine on it. Do not do any of these things. Simply follow the instructions in this book or the submission guidelines for the particular magazine, nothing else.

✎ Write grammatically perfect query text. Some people think that grammar rules do not apply to email. They do in professional correspondence. When you are pitching a story to an editor, your email is your business card. If your query is not perfect, why should they think your story would be any different? Check and double-check your email before clicking Send.

Cultivate Relationships

Relationships have value that may increase over time. Some of the first articles I ever sold were to an editor at *Blue Water Sailing*. A couple years later, I noticed her name in the *Cruising World* masthead. I checked her LinkedIn profile and saw that indeed, she had made the switch.

She was at the bottom of the list of *Cruising World* editors, but nonetheless, when I was ready to pitch my first feature story to *Cruising World*, I sent my query to this editor. I reminded her who I was, that she'd bought a couple pieces from me as a *Blue Water Sailing* editor, and offered her my story. She got right back to me, warmly recalling that we had worked together before and confirming that she was not in the position to buy a *Cruising World* feature, but offering to forward my query in-house. My story sold. I know that my connection with this editor helped to keep my query from being buried in the slush pile or otherwise lost in the shuffle. Today, the former *Blue Water Sailing* junior editor is a senior editor at *Cruising World,* and someone I regard as a friendly colleague.

Pitching the Query

As I wrote above, always address your query to a specific person, never "To Whom It May Concern" or "Editor." How do you determine which editor to name?

The masthead is the primary resource for making this determination. This resource is a part of every magazine—usually a part of the front matter (but is often not included on a magazine's website). In corporate-owned magazines, there may be two mastheads, used to distinguish the corporate folks from the magazine-specific folks. You can always ignore the corporate masthead.

In the masthead, magazines list their staff hierarchically, with the editorial boss always listed first. (The title for this role varies by magazine. You may see executive editor, editor-in-chief, editor, editor & publisher, founder/editor.) Ignore the art, design, and advertising staff; focus on the editors.

Single-Editor Mags

No, in this section I am not commenting on the marital status of any editor. Rather, I am letting you know that when there is only one editor listed on a magazine's masthead (as will be the case for many smaller magazines), that is the person to whom you should address your query.

Multiple-Editor Mags

Most magazines staff multiple editors. Determining which editor to address your query to is not always straightforward. Before I get into choosing an editor, let me offer this: Unless you are pitching a full-length feature story, resist the temptation to address your query to the editorial boss. In an article published in the *WritersWeekly* e-zine, Janene Mascarella wrote that sending your query to the editor listed at the top of the masthead is like, "looking for a job in Washington and sending your resume to the president of the United States." Mascarella then acknowledges that this is an extreme parallel, but otherwise very true. You should aim to pitch a more appropriate editor.

Look at the names of the editors listed below the boss. They will have titles such as deputy editor, associate editor, senior editor, managing editor, and assistant editor. This is the pool from which you should select a person to contact.

SAIL magazine currently lists nine editors and their titles in the following order (as well as 8 people listed under Contributing Editor):

EDITOR-IN-CHIEF
EXECUTIVE EDITOR
SENIOR EDITOR
WEB EDITOR
CRUISING EDITOR
RACING EDITOR
TECHNICAL EDITOR
ELECTRONICS EDITOR
EDITOR-AT-LARGE

This list is particularly long, but very helpful to the freelance writer. If you came up with a cruising story that you thought would be a good fit for the Cruising Under Sail section of *SAIL* magazine, and you'd never sold a story to *SAIL* magazine, to which editor would you send your query? Yeah, the Cruising Editor would be a good bet.

Unfortunately, few boating magazines feature a list of such aptly named editors. What if the magazine to which you are interested in selling your cruising story lists non-descript editor titles in their masthead? This is more common than not. Look at the editorial roster of *Cruising World* magazine:

EDITOR
EXECUTIVE EDITOR
SENIOR EDITOR
MANAGING EDITOR
ELECTRONICS EDITOR
DIGITAL EDITOR
COPY EDITOR

It would seem that all you could discern from this list is that any electronics-related story you would pitch to the Electronics Editor—and that would be wrong. I happen to know that the Electronics Editor, Digital Editor, and Copy Editor do not work with writers directly. So what do you do?

In the absence of hard rules, I recommend using the following guidelines.

- If you previously sold a story to the magazine in question, send your new query to the same editor you dealt with before, without regard to other considerations. If that person hands you off to another editor, great, now you have two contacts at that magazine and I hope you are developing a sense of which editor handles which types of stories and you can direct future pitches accordingly.

- How long do you think your story will be? If you are pitching a 2,500-word feature, this may be an occasion to send it to the first- or second-listed editor. Generally, regardless of subject, features are considered and bought by editors with more experience and authority. Accordingly, if you are pitching a 200-word helpful tip, consider addressing your query to the junior editor.

- Where do you see your story fitting between the covers of the magazine? Most magazines are organized into sections and sometimes that is a good clue. *Cruising World* includes a section titled, "Underway." On the first page of this section, in every issue, Jen Brett is listed as the editor. If you decide to pitch *Cruising World* and think your story belongs in the "Underway" section, Jen Brett is the person to whom you would send your query (Brett is currently listed in the *Cruising World* masthead as the Senior Editor, below the Editor and Executive Editor).

✎ Pick up the phone. Most of the magazines I know list a phone number for their editorial office in their masthead. Call and ask who the appropriate editor is to receive your query.

If you are still not sure to whom you should address your query, do not stress about it. For the half-dozen magazines I sell my writing to regularly, for the ones that list several editors, I am usually corresponding with the third-listed editor for stories in the front-of-book and the second- or first-listed editor for features. Simply address your query to a mid-level editor on the masthead and trust that if they are not the correct editor, they will forward your pitch.

The Address

Once you determine a specific person to whom you want to address your query, how do you determine their email address? Usually, magazines do not publish staff email addresses. Rather, a magazine will specify in their submission guidelines a generic address they want writers to use for sending queries (such as submissions@boatmag.com). Even if you are able to sleuth the email address of a particular editor—even if a magazine publishes the individual addresses of its staff editors—pay attention to submission guidelines and use the specified address. Once you get a response from a specific editor, you can use their email address for future correspondence and queries.

Even if you are able to sleuth the email address of a particular editor—even if a magazine publishes the individual addresses of its staff editors—pay attention to submission guidelines and use the specified address.

Pitching Simultaneously

Other than the exception noted below, never pitch the same story to multiple editors at the same time. If an editor passes on your story, that is the time to pitch it to an editor at another magazine, not before. In the rare case you do not hear back from an editor you queried (and a couple weeks have passed with no response to the follow-up email you sent a month after pitching), feel free to send a polite email letting them know that you'd like to remove your query from consideration so that you may send it to another magazine. Then do just that (and consider whether that is an editor you want to query first in the future).

An exception to this rule is simultaneously pitching the same story to two publications in very different markets. If you are very confident no competitive overlap exists between the publications, go ahead and query both. However, in both cases, be sure to add a note in your query indicating that you are simultaneously pitching a non-competing publication (indicating the name of the publication and the market).

I once wrote a story about British solo non-stop circumnavigator Jeanne Socrates. She was beginning and ending her circumnavigation in Victoria, B.C. I knew the Canadian regional magazine, *Pacific Yachting*, would be interested, but I also figured a U.K. magazine would like a story about their hometown girl. I pitched the story to *Pacific Yachting* and *Yachting Monthly* simultaneously—same story, same pics—and let both editors know I was querying the other.

Post Pitch

You can expect to wait. Sometimes you will catch an editor when they are reviewing queries and get a response immediately. Other times, weeks will pass with no word. The latter scenario is the norm, get used to it. When you do get an emailed response, it will probably fit into one of the following four response types:

🖊 **"We'd like to buy your story."** In the best-case scenario, an editor will get back to you with an offer to buy your story. Most of the time, this will include the price they are willing to pay and the terms of payment—either upon acceptance or upon publication. The editor may also specify other conditions, such as a word count not to exceed or a date by which they want your story delivered.

🖊 **"Please send us your story on spec."** This is a great response because it means you have come up with a great idea. It means the editor is interested in buying a well-written story based on your idea; they are just not willing to commit to buying that story at this point. In other words, "Feel free to write and send your story, your idea sounds good, but I'm not guaranteeing you I'll buy it." An editor may do this because either 1) they can imagine a great story coming from your idea, but are not confident that you are able to write it, or 2) they have faith in your writing ability, but aren't certain your idea can be turned into a story they want to buy. Either way, they have opened the door and invited you in to show them what you can do. When an editor gives you the green light to deliver something on spec, all you have to do is write the story you promised and make it shine.

🖊 **"I liked this idea, but..."** This may be the introduction to a counter. The editor sort of likes where your story idea is headed, but maybe is not sure about it and is offering some recommendations or critique. This is usually an invitation to you to modify your idea according to the editor's response, and then to pitch your modified idea. Do your best to deliver what they want, but only if the new idea is still a story you're able to write and are interested in writing.

✎ **"We're gonna pass."** Get used to rejection, but do not let it get you down. If an editor politely turns down your story idea, they will probably also let you know why. A rejection often has nothing to do with the quality of your pitch. It may be because the editor ran a similar story three months before (you should have known this…) or has a similar story on tap for a pending issue (editors often work far into the future, buying stories that will not be published for many months down the road). By the way, if an editor passes on your story, never submit it to another editor at the same magazine. Consider that any editor who turns down your story is speaking for the entire publication.

If more than a month passes and you have not received a response, take a good look at your query. Was it professional? Did you send it to the right editor? Editors are busy and work in monthly cycles. They may devote some weeks to getting an issue to the printer on deadline, putting off evaluating and responding to queries for another time in the month. For this reason, if you hear nothing and you know you sent it to the right person, feel free to send a gentle reminder email, but wait at least one month before doing so.

Keep Your Head Up

At some point, an editor will reject your query (and if you stick with it, many editors will reject many of your queries). It may be that your story idea and query were great and that you pitched the right person, but that the magazine could not run your story at this time for reasons that are totally out of your control and that could not be foreseen. Or it may be that your story idea was unappealing, that your query was weak, or that you pitched the wrong person. You may never know why, but you will be rejected.

Move on. If selling your writing is still your goal, do not be daunted. Do not think you are not good enough.

Boating writer Gary "Cap'n Fatty" Goodlander offers a great story on his website that is a must-read for every aspiring freelance writer. He titled it, "Writing to Stay Afloat" (www.fattygoodlander.com/writers_only). He tells his story of getting started selling his writing. He highlights the work and persistence that may be necessary to hone your craft, to hone your approach, and ultimately, to sell your writing. Goodlander wrote and failed to sell 16 stories without giving up (he had set a goal to receive 100 rejection letters).

> *"'These aren't rejections,' I'd tell myself. 'These are visible reminders that I'm continuously searching for the markets which will eventually buy my work on a regular basis!'"*

The Submission

S ubmission time! The hard part is over. You came up with a great story idea, pitched it successfully, and now you have a magazine editor waiting eagerly to read your writing. All that remains to do is to prep, format, and send everything off. Following is the information you need to do it right.

The Manuscript

I send every story manuscript as an attached document. Every editor I have worked with is accustomed to receiving story submissions as Microsoft Word documents. Even if you don't use Word to write your stories (consider AbiWord, Apple Pages, Google Docs, OpenOffice Writer, and Scrivener), it's a good idea to use a program that allows you to save your file in the .doc format (most of them do) and then submit it as a .doc file attachment.

The Manuscript File Name

I always name manuscript files using a specific format. I think it is important that the file name includes key information; the file may not always remain attached to your email. Feel free to copy the following format or find one that works for you.

    <LastName>_<MagazineNameOrInitials>_<ShortenedStoryTitle>.doc

In this way, a document file I'm submitting to *Cruising World* magazine that is a story about cruising French Polynesia's Marquesas island group that I've titled, "May in the Marquesas," would be named:

    Robertson_CW_Marquesas.doc

The text of any related sidebars (two of them in this example) should be contained in separate files and you should name these files using the same name and format, but appended.

    Robertson_CW_Marquesas_SIDEBAR_1_of_2.doc

The Manuscript Layout

Layout is critical. You need to present your words in a way that is professional and comfortable for the editor (what she is used to seeing). Following are my suggestions from the simple document layout that has worked well for me.

Remember to keep text formatting plain and minimal. It's okay to put specific words in italic, but avoid different fonts and text sizes (even for the title, if you include a title—editors always choose their own title anyway), fancy spacing, footnoting, etc.

As I wrote earlier, for stories under 200 words or so, I attach them in a distinct document, but to aid the editor, I also include the same text in the body of the email.

The Photos

Never mix your words and photos. Do not copy or insert photos in your manuscript to show the editor, "how nicely the pictures will look with my text," or to give them, "ideas about how to design the article." Never. Don't do it.

Okay, that said, what is the best way to send an editor the large photo files you are submitting with your story? We will get to that; first, I have a couple additional admonitions:

🖋 Never send photos to an editor before they request them. Your query should reference the photos you have to accompany your story ("I have terrific photos to accompany my story"), but wait to send them until the editor asks to see them.

🖋 Only attach photos to an email if the total size of the attachments is less than 10MB. (This is arbitrary, a rule of thumb I use. I do not think any more than this is professional and some email systems will reject emails in excess of 10MB.)

Never mix your words and photos.

Anticipating you'll have a large selection of large photo files to accompany your story submission, some magazine editors may give you a file transfer protocol (FTP) site address to which you can simply upload your photos (and from which they can access your photos). In fact, if they do not offer, before submitting a requested story it is appropriate to ask the editor whether they have an FTP site to which you can upload your photos. If the magazine does not have a designated FTP site, you should set up your own such solution. Any of the many cloud-based file storage services should work.

I have long used Microsoft's OneDrive, the free cloud-based file storage solution associated with my Hotmail/Outlook email address. I upload manuscripts and photos there, all organized in folders by magazine and story. When it is time to submit photos to a magazine editor, I simply use the service to create a link to the particular folder. When I send that link to an editor (via email), all that editor has to do is click that link to access all the files in that particular folder. (However, I am careful to create the correct type of link—OneDrive will create either a link that allows the link recipient to view, but not download or edit the files, or one that allows the recipient full access to the files.)

Other services work the same way. Dropbox is perhaps the most popular and I have used it successfully to collaborate with two other writers simultaneously. Dropbox is currently free to use so long as your space needs do not exceed 2 GB.

If you are a Gmail user or do all your work within Apple's ecosystem, you will find similar, free, cloud-based solutions available to you.

Another thing an editor (or designer) will appreciate is a photo key—a list or table or spreadsheet that gives descriptions of your photos (by file name) and

When you are ready to reply, keep it brief. Do not over-think this step.

in cases where not all of the photos were taken by the writer, identifies the photographer. Keep your descriptions brief—perhaps identifying only geographic place names or animal types or people in the photos (when they are referenced in the story). Unless you are writing for a photography magazine, an editor will neither need nor request photo metadata (camera and lens specs and settings).

When I submit more than a few dozen photos for a story (knowing the editor will choose fewer than 10 photos), I usually let the editor know that I've held off on making a key until they've whittled the list down, selecting the photos they intend to use. Note: Some magazines want to see all the photos that you think are publishable. Others set clear limits in their writer's guidelines, requesting that you submit no more than a dozen photos, for example. If you are in doubt about what to send, ask the editor.

The Email

Always find the email the editor last sent you, the one requesting your manuscript, and reply to that email, rather than creating a new one. This helps keep the flow of information organized in the editor's email inbox so that they remember who you are and that this is a story they requested. I have had editors request this of me specifically.

When you are ready to reply, keep it brief. Do not over-think this step. Following is an example.

Hi Karen,

Attached are two files: the Replacing Wooden Hatches manuscript you requested of me, and a photo key. Please use the following link to access 14 high-res photos I took to illustrate the story.

<link>

Please let me know if you need anything else. I look forward to hearing from you.

Michael Robertson

Post-Submission

Congratulations! You got some love from an editor who expressed interest in your story and you have sent them your baby. Now you are checking your email every hour, eager for a response. I hope that the editor will get back to you quickly, at least to let you know he got it. However, you may hear nothing. Be patient. As with a query, wait at least a month before sending a follow up email regarding your submission. Ultimately, you will get a response, this is a submission they requested of you.

✐ **Acceptance:** If you submitted your story on spec, now is when the editor will quote you a price for your story and pictures. Congratulations! Get back to the editor right away letting them know the terms are acceptable (see the section below, Can I negotiate?). Some magazines (especially the corporate-owned magazines) will not publish your work until you have signed a contract giving them the rights to do so. If this is one of those magazines, you should expect an emailed contract soon after you agree to the emailed terms. You have nothing else to do but to make sure the dollar amount in the contract agrees with the amount you were quoted, sign it, and send it back—either via postal mail or scanned and sent via email.

✐ **Revisions:** Sometimes an editor will return a story to you for specific revisions. Read the editor's feedback carefully, ask any follow up questions to be clear on what she is requesting, and then fix your story. Editors appreciate working with responsive, cooperative writers.

✐ **Rejection:** It is possible for an editor to flat-out reject a story they invited you to submit on spec, but unlikely. If they invited you to submit the story, it is because they like the idea and want to see the story in their magazine. If they feel you have not developed your idea into the story they envisioned, more often than not, they will ask you to revise it. However, if they don't see promise in your writing or if things have changed in their business from the time they requested the story and the time you delivered, they may reject your submission. If this happens, they will likely explain why. If they don't, feel free to follow up; you are owed an explanation at this point.

After you submit your story and the editor accepts it, it is time to wait, again. It could take months (even a year) for the issue to come out that features your work. It is okay to ask an editor in which issue they plan to run your piece (and it may be reflected in your contract, if you were asked to sign one), but don't keep asking if it doesn't appear in the scheduled issue. Remember, editors are busy people you want in your corner. Oftentimes editors shuffle stories and your work may appear a couple issues sooner or later than planned. Just watch for it, I know you are eager.

The Money

In case nobody told you—maybe I should have mentioned this earlier in this book—you are unlikely to get rich selling your writing to niche market magazines. I recommend your motivation come from your strong interest in your niche (because your story payment will not include expenses), from your enjoyment of writing, and from the validation you get from being paid for your writing. Personally, all these things motivate me equally *and* I do it for the money. But you have to know that as a sailboat cruising family, we enjoy a relatively low cost of living and we're living off our savings. Over the past few years, I have averaged roughly 30 hours per week writing. Of those 30 hours, I devote only 5-7 to magazine writing. The rest of my writing time (and writing time includes researching, picture taking, and corresponding) I spend blogging and book writing. I am not (yet) earning enough writing income to support our family of four, but I am able to significantly stem the outflow from our savings).

The Art of the Deal

It's embarrassing to think about now, but when I sold my first-ever magazine story to *SAIL* magazine back in 2005, I thought I would be a chump to accept the first payment the editor offered me (and looking back from 2016, the $900 she offered was very good, totally in-line with the market and my experience). After all, as of this sale, I was a professional writer and I aimed to be a savvy professional writer. By that time, I had read that negotiating was not a step in the process, but I didn't accept it.

When the editor accepted my story and offered me payment, I thanked her and countered. "You're terms are mostly acceptable, but I'd like *SAIL* to sweeten the deal [yeah, I wrote "sweeten the deal"] by including a copy of Peter Neilson's new book, *Sailpower: Trim and Techniques for Cruising Sailors.*" (Peter Neilson was her boss.) The editor responded patiently, explaining that Peter's book was not a part of her offer and asking if I wanted to withdraw my story from consideration.

"No," I responded, "I accept your original terms. Thank you."

Don't be like I was.

I am not anti-negotiation, and I am not suggesting you kowtow because you are getting started. In my experience, buyers (editors) and sellers (writers) in the niche-market magazine business do not negotiate the payments for individual story sales. The editor is willing to pay you a certain amount for your story. This amount is likely based in part on how the editor perceives your experience, in part on your name recognition to the market (are you famous in your niche?), and in part on the section for which your story is intended and the length of your story.

That said, if you are submitting your third book review with the same editor, for example, and you think the editor is pleased with what you are delivering, it would not hurt to ask if they would consider a higher rate for future reviews.

> *As a writer, I exert market forces when I choose where to pitch my story idea.*

I am sure Christopher Hitchens (or rather, his agent) negotiated his fees with *Vanity Fair* and I am sure Adam Gopnik does the same with *The New Yorker*. Yet do not confuse the mass-market magazines with the niche-market magazines. (And do not confuse yourself with established, very-in-demand writers—not yet anyway.)

Some magazines' websites list the fixed amounts they pay for stories (and photos) based on the section of the magazine in which they plan to run the story. *Good Old Boat* and *Cruising Outpost* are two in my market that feature a menu of payment amounts on their site.

So what market forces are at work if editors are not willing to negotiate and some magazines publish a fixed payment schedule?

The Market

Not all magazines pay the same rates. As a writer, I exert market forces when I choose where to pitch my story idea. If I come up with an idea for a feature-length story that would fit equally well in the pages of *Blue Water Sailing, Cruising Outpost, Cruising World,* and *SAIL.* I alone decide where to pitch it.

I know that if I sell my story to one of the higher-circulation magazines—*Cruising World* or *SAIL*—the editor will pay more (and more people will read my story). I know that if I sell my story to one of the lower-circulation magazines—*Blue Water Sailing* or *Cruising Outpost*—the editor will pay less (and fewer people will read my story). Accordingly, with no other factors at play, I will send my query first to one of the higher-paying editors. If they pass on my pitch, I can always send it to a lower-paying editor. Ostensibly, for magazines targeting the same readership, the highest-paying editors are getting the most desirable content.

Because higher-circulation magazines tend to pay more, the competition for selling a story may be greater (and the inverse is not necessarily true—there may be stiff competition to get a story accepted by a lower-circulation, lower-paying magazine that writers like and want to sell to). Yet do not be dissuaded from pitching editors at the higher-circulation national glossies simply because you are starting out and think you are not yet 'that good.' I hope that you are putting forth the effort and turning out writing you are proud of and that can stand up. If you are not, keep at it because the bigger players in the niche market regularly publish good stories from new writers.

How much can I earn?

The limiting factor affecting your earnings as a freelance writer is the number of saleable ideas you can come up with. I have earned $400 for 300-word stories that took me 4 hours to write. Extrapolating, I should be able to work 2 hours a day, 5 days a week and make $52,000 a year, pre-taxes, writing and selling stories for magazines. However, how often do I get saleable ideas for 300-word stories I can write in 4 hours and sell for $400? Not often.

Following are approximate amounts you can expect to be paid for the stories you sell that come from the good ideas you get. The ranges come from the variance in boating magazine pay rates; as I wrote earlier, some pay much more than others. In addition, you may be willing to write for free to get your first bylines and there are plenty of pubs willing to pay that rate. I have not included zero in the ranges below. Accordingly, these numbers are probably too imprecise to be of any real value. However, for what they're worth...

A feature-length story (with photos) might earn you $250 at the bottom of the range and $2,000 at the top. A 100-word book review might earn $20-$100. A cover photo might earn $100-$750. A 300-word news report (with photos) might be worth $50-$400.

Keep in mind that while most magazines do not pay by the word (*Ocean Navigator* is the only magazine that has ever paid me by the word), word count is a factor. A longer story (especially a feature) with lots of quality photos will earn you a much larger payment than a short snippet sold to the same magazine. However, know that longer stories are a *lot* more work, and that you will usually earn more for shorter pieces for the time you spend. Of course, an idea is an idea. Whether you come up with an idea for a feature, or an idea for a short piece, is probably not something you control. Take every idea that excites you, and run with it.

Appendix: Boating Mag Market

Media companies own the highest-circulation boating magazines in the U.S. Each of these companies publish several, even dozens, of titles in and out of the boating market.

- **Bonnier Corp.** is an American magazine publisher owned by a Swedish parent company. They publish over 40 titles in the U.S. and their boating titles include *Boating*, *Cruising World*, *Power Cruising*, *Sailing World*, and *Yachting*.

- **Active Interest Media** is a publisher of over 40 niche-market magazines. Their boating titles include *SAIL*, *PassageMaker*, *Power&Motoryacht*, and *Soundings*.

- **Duncan McIntosh Company** is a relatively small house, publishing only *Sea*, *Boating World*, *The Log*, and one non-boating magazine.

- In the UK, the large media corporation **Time, Inc.** publishes *Yachting Monthly*, *Practical Boat Owner*, and *Yachting World*.

- Along with several consumer magazines, Australia's **Yaffa Media** publishes two boating titles: *Cruising Helmsman* and *Sailing + Yachting*

Though this ownership distinction is largely lost on readers, as a freelance boating writer you should have a sense of this structure. Not only because these company names will appear on your check, but because very often the editor of one title will also have an editorial position at another in-house title.

As a writer, there are three minor differences between selling to a corporate-owned magazine and an independent:

✎ The corporations own the highest-circulation magazines in the boating market. Usually, higher-circulation magazines pay more than lower-circulation magazines.

✎ The corporate-owned magazines usually pay upon acceptance vs. paying upon publication.

✎ The corporate-owned magazines will usually require the writer to sign and return a formal contract, whereas most of the independently owned magazines are less formal.

However, the boating magazine market is much larger than the 17 corporate-owned titles I listed above. Following is a list of the titles (corporate- and independently-owned) I consider for my story ideas (even this is not a comprehensive list of the magazines in this niche).

38 Boating Magazine Profiles

North American Boating Magazines (approximate circulations*)

Blue Water Sailing (50,000) **CONTENT:** nearly any story related to sailboat cruising. **$:** lower end. **COMPARE TO:** *Cruising World, Cruising Helmsman* **SUBMISSION EMAIL:** kira@bwsailing.com

Boating (150,000) **CONTENT:** Powerboaters of all types. **$:** higher end. **COMPARE TO:** *Boating World* **SUBMISSION EMAIL:** editor@boatigmag.com

Boating World (150,000) **CONTENT:** Recreational trailerboating. **$:** higher end. **COMPARE TO:** *Boating* **SUBMISSION EMAIL:** <online submission form>

BoatU.S. (500,000) **CONTENT:** Recreational boating, all facets, emphasis on inshore. **$:** higher end. **COMPARE TO:** Some overlap with *Boating, Boating World, Cruising World, SAIL* **SUBMISSION EMAIL:** magazine@BoatUS.com

Cruising Outpost (35,000) **CONTENT:** Focus on the lifestyle aspects of sail and trawler cruising. **$:** lower end. **COMPARE TO:** Some overlap with *PassageMaker, Latitude 38, Blue Water Sailing* **SUBMISSION EMAIL:** submissions@cruisingoutpost.com

Cruising World (100,000) **CONTENT:** nearly any story related to sailboat cruising. **$:** higher end. **COMPARE TO:** *Blue Water Sailing, Cruising Helmsman,* some overlap with *SAIL*
SUBMISSION EMAIL: editors@CruisingWorld.com

Good Old Boat (25,000) **CONTENT:** DIY technical regarding fiberglass boats from the 70s through the 00's. Also includes essays from writers about their good old boats. **$:** lower end.
SUBMISSION EMAIL: karen@goodoldboat.com

Latitude 38 (40,000) **CONTENT:** Stories related to Bay Area sailing news, regional sailing info (racing, recreation, and cruising from the West Coast of North America between San Francisco and Puerto Vallarta), and worldwide sailboat cruising. **$:** lower end.
SUBMISSION EMAIL: editorial@latitude38.com

Ocean Navigator (40,000) **CONTENT:** Worldwide voyaging, under sail or power. **$:** mid-range.
SUBMISSION EMAIL: tqueeney@oceannavigator.com

PassageMaker (30,000) **CONTENT:** Trawlers, lifestyle and destination cruising. **$:** low-range. **COMPARE TO:** Some overlap with *Power&Motoryacht, Cruising Outpost*
SUBMISSION EMAIL: mfusco@passagemaker.com

Power&Motoryacht (100,000) **CONTENT:** Everything about recreational powerboats 24 feet and larger. **$:** mid-range.
SUBMISSION EMAIL: jwood@aimmedia.com

Professional Boatbuilder (20,000) **CONTENT:** Focuses on materials, design, and construction techniques and repair solutions chosen by boatbuilders, repairers, designers, and surveyors. **$:** UNK
SUBMISSION EMAIL: paul.lazarus@proboat.com

SAIL (100,000) **CONTENT:** nearly any story related to sailing—a mix of racing, recreation, cruising, technical. **$:** higher end. **COMPARE TO:** *Sailing World, Yachting Monthly, Sailing.*
SUBMISSION EMAIL: sailmail@sailmagazine.com

Sailing (40,000) **CONTENT:** nearly any story related to sailing—a mix of racing, recreation, cruising, technical. **$:** higher end. **COMPARE TO:** *Sailing World, Yachting Monthly, SAIL.*
SUBMISSION EMAIL: editorial@sailingmagazine.net

Sailing World (30,000) **CONTENT:** nearly any story related to sailing—a mix of racing, recreation, cruising, technical. **$:** higher end. **COMPARE TO:** *SAIL, Yachting Monthly, Sailing.*
SUBMISSION EMAIL: editor@SailingWorld.com

Soundings (40,000) **CONTENT:** Recreational boating, covering issues, events, seamanship, how-to, gear and cruising destinations. **$:** UNK
SUBMISSION EMAIL: editorial@soundingspub.com

WoodenBoat (70,000) **CONTENT:** Everything wooden boat: for owners, builders, and designers. **$:** lower end
SUBMISSION EMAIL: <online submission form>

Yachting: (100,000) **CONTENT:** Everything related to ownership, maintenance, and enjoyment of premium yachts (power). **$:** UNK
COMPARE TO: Some overlap with *Power&Motoryacht*
SUBMISSION EMAIL: editor@yachtigmagazie.com

Regional Boating Magazines (Regional focus)

48 North (U.S. Pacific Northwest)
SUBMISSION EMAIL: joe@48north.com

Chesapeake Bay Magazine (Chesapeake Bay)
SUBMISSION EMAIL: editor@ChesapeakeBoating.net

Great Lakes Boating (waterways in the Great Lakes region)
SUBMISSION EMAIL: <online submission form, or call: 312.266.8400>

Lakeland Boating (waterways in the Great Lakes region)
SUBMISSION EMAIL: staff@lakelandboating.com

Latitude 38 (worldwide, with emphasis on San Francisco and U.S. West Coast)—see profile under North American Boating Magazines
SUBMISSION EMAIL: editorial@latitude38.com

Maine Boats, Homes & Harbors (Maine)
SUBMISSION EMAIL: editor@maineboats.com

Pacific Yachting (British Columbia and U.S. Pacific Northwest)—see listing under Foreign English-Language Boating Magazines
SUBMISSION EMAIL: editor@pacificyachting.com

Sea (Western U.S.—regional editions for California and the Pacific Northwest)
SUBMISSION EMAIL: <online submission form>

Southern Boating (Southeast U.S., Gulf of Mexico, Bahamas, and Caribbean)
SUBMISSION EMAIL: liz@southernboating.com

Spinsheet (Chesapeake Bay)
SUBMISSION EMAIL: molly@Spinsheet.com

The Log (California)
SUBMISSION EMAIL: <online submission form>

Three Sheets Northwest (online magazine covering the U.S. Pacific Northwest)
SUBMISSION EMAIL: <online submission form>

Foreign English-Language Boating Magazines (Country)

Afloat (Ireland)
SUBMISSION EMAIL: <online submission form>

All At Sea (U.K.)
SUBMISSION EMAIL: editor@allatsea.co.uk

Canadian Yachting (Canada)
SUBMISSION EMAIL: aadams@kerrwil.com

Cruising Helmsman (Australia)
SUBMISSION EMAIL: philross@yaffa.com.au

Boating NZ (New Zealand)
SUBMISSION EMAIL: editor@boatingnz.co.nz

Pacific Yachting (Canada)
SUBMISSION EMAIL: editor@pacificyachting.com

Practical Boat Owner (U.K)
SUBMISSION EMAIL: pbo@timeinc.com

Sailing + Yachting (Australia)
SUBMISSION EMAIL: kimberleywilmot@yaffa.com.au

Yachting Monthly (U.K.)
  SUBMISSION EMAIL: yachtingmonthly@timeinc.com

Yachting World (U.K.)
  SUBMISSION EMAIL: elaine.bunting@timeinc.com

* For more information about circulation data, refer to the Alliance for Audited Media site: http://auditedmedia.com/resources/guides-and-evaluation-forms/consumer-magazines/

One More Thing

Once you have sold a story you are proud of, consider joining Boating Writers International (BWI). This is an organization of writers (mostly freelance) and others who work in boating journalism. The organization disseminates knowledge via a newsletter and offers networking opportunities. However, during the years I have been a member, the most value from my membership has come from the annual writing contest.

BWI organizes and sponsors the only marine-market-specific writing competition. Annually, the organization awards cash prizes in seventeen different categories for work published during the preceding year. Membership (currently $50 dues paid annually) includes two free entries to the contest. This is the only opportunity I know of to be recognized and awarded for your boat-related published writing—a great addition to a freelancer's resume.

Additionally, some magazines (I know *Cruising World* has done this) may sponsor your BWI membership for the year you have written stories for them. They may even take care of packaging and submitting your entries from your stories published in their magazine.

For more information, go to www.bwi.org

There is no more.

       Now go write.

            It's not magic, it's work.

                  You can do it.

Index

.doc, 78
48 North, 92
AbiWord, 78
acceptance, 83
Active Interest Media, 89
Afloat, 93
All At Sea, 93
Apple Pages, 78
article, 4
artwork, 4
back of book, 4
Biles, Paula, 53
Blue Water Sailing, 22, 34, 36, 69, 87, 90, 91
Boating, 22, 37, 89, 90
Boating NZ, 93
Boating World, 89, 90
Boating Writers International, 94
BoatU.S., 22, 23, 34, 35, 36, 90
Bonnier Corp., 89
book, 4
book review, 24
Brett, Jen, 72
byline, 4, 18, 27
Calder, Nigel, 29
Canadian Yachting, 93
Casey, Don, 30
Cheever, John, 39

Chesapeake Bay Magazine, 35, 92
Chiles, Webb, 55
circulation, 4
Classic Plastic, 26
clean copy, 5
column, 5
communicating with an editor, 36, 65, 66, 67, 82
copyright, 5
Creative Knitting, 22
Cruising Helmsman, 89, 90, 91, 93
Cruising Outpost, 36, 86, 87, 90, 91
Cruising World, 11, 14, 15, 22, 23, 26, 32, 34, 36, 55, 60, 64, 65, 69, 71, 72, 78, 87, 89, 90, 91, 94
D'Antonio, Steve, 29
Doane, Charles, 36
dpi, 59
Dropbox, 81
Duncan McIntosh Company, 89
editing, 44
editor, 5
environmental slant, 22
feature, 3, 5, 9, 12, 16, 17, 18, 22, 23, 33, 34, 38, 41, 43, 44,

47, 49, 55, 58, 69, 70, 71, 72, 86, 87, 88
file transfer protocol (also see FTP), 80
First North American Rights, 5
food related, 22
foreign payment, 38
formatting a manuscript, 79
Fortune, 37
front matter, 6
front of book, 6
FTP (also see file transfer protocol), 80
Good Old Boat, 15, 17, 18, 24, 26, 33, 34, 53, 64, 65, 86, 91
Goodlander, Gary "Cap'n Fatty", 77
Google Docs, 78
Gopnik, Adam, 86
Great Lakes Boating, 92
Green Wakes, 22
Hitches, Christopher, 86
ideas for story, 10
interviewing, 19, 20
Johnson, Sara Dawn, 46
JPEG, 25, 51, 61
kill fee, 6
King, Stephen, 44
Lakeland Boating, 92
Larson, Karen, 65
Latitude 38, 34, 90, 91, 92
Loranca, Tanya, 60
Maine Boats, Homes & Harbors, 92
manuscript, 6
Mascarella, Janene, 70
masthead, 6
media kit, 6

megapixel, 57, 61
membership magazine, 35
Model Railroader, 2, 3
naming files, 78
negotiating payment, 85
Neilson, Peter, 85
niche-market, 1
Ocean Navigator, 13, 30, 34, 88, 91
on spec, 7, 20, 37, 42, 75, 83
OneDrive, 81
OpenOffice Writer, 78
OrganicLife, 24
over the transom, 7
Pacific Yachting, 14, 22, 33, 34, 37, 38, 47, 64, 65, 74, 92, 93
PassageMaker, 89, 90, 91
Pawlik-Kienlen, Laurie, 2
PDF, 25
People, 2
photos, 14, 21, 22, 23, 24, 27, 39, 47, 50, 60, 80, 81, 82, 86, 88
photos, journalistic, 54
photos, manipulation, 51
photos, technical, 52
photos, two types, 52
piece, 7
pitch, 7, 8, 14, 15, 26, 28, 29, 30, 41, 62, 74, 76, 78
pixels, 57, 58, 59, 60, 61
polarizing filter, 50, 53
Popular Science, 2
Power Cruising, 89
Power&Motoryacht, 89, 91, 92
Powerboat Cruising, 22
ppi, 57, 58, 59, 60
Practical Boat Owner, 93

product reviews, 25
Professional Boatbuilder, 91
pull quote, 7
query, 8, 11, 13, 14, 27, 30, 36,
    40, 41, 42, 43, 47, 62, 63, 65,
    66, 67, 68, 69, 70, 71, 72, 73,
    74, 76, 80, 82, 87
rejection, 76, 83
revision, 83
royalties, 8
SAIL, 8, 12, 16, 18, 22, 23, 33,
    34, 35, 36, 37, 47, 64, 65, 71,
    85, 87, 89, 90, 91, 92
Sailing, 91
Sailing + Yachting, 89, 93
Sailing Anarchy, 18
Sailing for Dummies, 40
Sailing World, 89, 92
*Sailpower--Trim and
    Techniques for Cruising
    Sailors*, 85
Sail-World, 18
Schulte, Pat, 56
Scrivener, 78
Scuttlebutt Sailing News, 18
Sea, 89, 93
section, 8
Selkirk, Diane, 40, 68
sending photos, 80
Sherman, Ed, 29

sidebar, 8, 78
Small Boats Monthly, 19
Socrates, Jeanne, 19, 74
Soundings, 92
Southern Boating, 93
Spinsheet, 93
SSCA Commodore's Bulletin, 18
story, 8
story idea, 10
The Atlantic, 2
The Log, 89, 93
The New Yorker, 86
Three Sheets Northwest, 19, 93
Time, Inc., 89
Underway, 11
upon acceptance, 9
upon publication, 9
upon submission, 9
Vanity Fair, 86
well, 9
Wired, 37
WoodenBoat, 92
word count, 9
writer's guidelines, 22, 33, 35,
    62, 82
Yachting, 92
Yachting Monthly, 2, 36, 37, 38,
    64, 65, 74, 89, 91, 92, 94
Yachting World, 89, 94
Yaffa Media, 89

About The Author

Michael Robertson was born and raised in Southern California. It was there that he spent an interminable decade earning a bachelor's degree in English from California State University Northridge, began messing about in boats, met a girl, went sailing with her, married her, and followed her cross-country to the District of Columbia. In D.C. they bought a house, built careers, and started a family. He had trouble finding time to write. After a decade, he and his wife ditched the house and careers and sailed away with their two daughters aboard their 40-foot sailboat, *Del Viento*. He's since done a lot of typing and sold his writing to boating magazines like *Blue Water Sailing, Cruising World, Good Old Boat, Latitude 38, Ocean Navigator, Pacific Yachting, SAIL,* and *Yachting Monthly.* He is co-author of *Voyaging With Kids: A guide to family life afloat* (2015, L&L Pardey Books).

Michael hopes to receive a flood of email (and Amazon reviews) from readers who successfully sold their writing after reading this book. He really hopes nobody ever has cause to write to tell him this book was not worth their reading time. In addition to writing, Michael is a freelance editor who works with writers on all types of projects, mostly nonfiction. dcwriteeditor@hotmail.com

<u>Notes:</u>

CPSIA information can be obtained
at www.ICGtesting.com
Printed in the USA
LVOW12s0213110717

540828LV00001B/167/P

9 780997 135800